REAL-TIME
DATA PROCESSING SYSTEMS:
INTRODUCTORY CONCEPTS

Prentice-Hall

Series in Automatic Computation

George Forsythe, Editor

PRENTICE-HALL INTERNATIONAL, INC., *London*
PRENTICE-HALL OF AUSTRALIA, PTY, LTD., *Sydney*
PRENTICE-HALL OF CANADA, LTD., *Toronto*
PRENTICE-HALL OF INDIA (PRIVATE) LTD., *New Delhi*
PRENTICE-HALL OF JAPAN, INC., *Tokyo*
PRENTICE-HALL DE MEXICO, S.A., *Mexico City*

REAL-TIME

DATA PROCESSING SYSTEMS:

INTRODUCTORY CONCEPTS

WILLIAM H. DESMONDE

Research Staff Member
IBM Corporation

PRENTICE-HALL, INC.
ENGLEWOOD CLIFFS, N. J.

Current printing (last digit):

12   11   10   9   8   7   6   5   4   3

Library of Congress Catalog Card No. 64-19676
Printed in the United States of America
76709 C

ACKNOWLEDGMENTS

I would like to thank the numerous individuals who have helped me gather material on real-time systems, either by discussing problems with me, or by furnishing me with reports and manuals.

In studying the Sabre project, I was aided by Roy V. Bigelow, John H. Brummer, Roy E. Cicale, William B. Elmore, M. Gerson Ginzberg, Robert V. Head, James L. Kessler, Alfred A. Scaia, John Siegfried, and Cecil P. Webb. I obtained information concerning other airline reservation systems from Glen Albers, Mrs. Barbara Allen, Francis M. DeKalb, Donald Liebelt, Edward D. Liljegren, Patrick A. Petty, and Robert Sobecki. On many topics, explanations by H. F. Scheuer were particularly helpful.

Robert L. Hoffman, John P. Lamb, and Gerald M. Weinberg gave me assistance in understanding Project Mercury. The diagram I use in the text for presenting the Mercury control program is adapted from a chart in Project Mercury final reports.

Much of the material relating to the Programmed Transmission Control is drawn from Nicholas Sternad's "Programming Considerations for the 7750" (*IBM Systems Journal*, March 1963) and other manuals prepared by Dr. Sternad.

A great deal of the information in the chapter on testing real-time systems is contained in a special report prepared by Charles Barbel, James Egglezos, James Martin, and Thomas P. Taylor. Glen Albers, Edward D. Liljegren, and G. M. Weinberg provided data on both the testing and planning of real-time systems.

I have drawn considerable material on file organization from writeups, classes, and seminars provided by the IBM Department of Education.

William R. Elmendorf has read a large part of the book, and has given me a number of useful suggestions. Numerous individuals within IBM reviewed portions of the manuscript and made helpful recommendations.

The material for this book was obtained from a wide variety of sources, over a long period of time. My apologies if I have forgotten to thank anyone for his assistance.

The development of real-time systems has been the result of the creativity and labor of a very large number of persons. It would be impossible for me to attempt in this book to cite all of the contributors, major and minor, to the projects I have discussed. The basic ideas in the Sabre control program were created by John Siegfried and James L. Kessler. Gerald M. Weinberg and Mrs. Marilyn Scott originated the multiprogramming monitor at Mercury. As stated in the text, Geoffrey Gordon developed the general-purpose simulation program which I have described.

TABLE OF CONTENTS

9 DISK FILE ORGANIZATION, 107

10 PLANNING AND MANAGING A REAL-TIME SYSTEM, 137

11 THE TESTING OF PROGRAMS IN REAL-TIME SYSTEMS, 151

12 THE OPTIMIZING OF SYSTEMS THROUGH SIMULATION, 161

REAL-TIME
DATA PROCESSING SYSTEMS:
INTRODUCTORY CONCEPTS

1 INTRODUCTION

PURPOSE OF BOOK

Electronic data processing is entering a new and dramatic phase. In the past, information has typically been gathered from large numbers of source documents, placed on punched cards, converted to magnetic tape, and then processed at some later date. A large time gap occurred between the origination of information and the printing of output documents. This procedure is satisfactory where an immediate response to a problem is not necessary, but is inadequate where rapid adjustments must be made to a large, fast-changing, complex situation.

To achieve a continual, dynamic interaction between a central processor and its environment, a *real-time* system is required. The number of such installations is increasing, and it is therefore becoming increasingly necessary for individuals in the data processing field to be familiar with real-time techniques. The aim of this book is to introduce the reader to many of the prevailing concepts.

It will be assumed that the reader is familiar with conventional programming. I will seek to avoid using any particular machine for explanations and illustrations. However, since two important real-time applications are using the IBM 7090, there will be a tendency for concepts unique to this computer to appear.

Practical problems in gathering information have caused me to confine my attention to IBM systems. From the limited material at my command when I prepared this manuscript, I have selected many of the most interesting details. But because of the immensity and diversity of the projects under way, and the rapid development of the technology, this book does not seek to be comprehensive or profound. Where equipment I have described has since been modified or replaced, the reader will nevertheless find it valuable to understand the functions which any equipment must perform to solve the necessary problems. I believe that this book will be useful both to students preparing to enter the data processing field and to professionals interested in large-scale Sabre-type applications. I must emphasize here that many of the complexities and great difficulties of Sabre-type systems are not present in numerous simple real-time applications.

To give the reader a glimpse into areas where real-time systems can and are being used, this introductory chapter describes briefly the overall characteristics of several applications.

THE MERCURY PROJECT

The exploration of outer space by manned vehicles furnishes a vivid illustration of a dynamic system requiring instantaneous surveillance and control by a communication-based computer. For example, the data processing system for Project Mercury† consisted basically of a single computer receiving input from and sending output to distant terminals and an operations control center. The computer was duplexed, but only one machine provided output at any given time. The extra computer was present in case of a machine failure in which case there was a switchover to the backup machine.

During the launching of a manned satellite, radar and telemetry data are sent to the computer. The computer must immediately calculate whether the spacecraft will be properly inserted into orbit. In all stages of a mission, the machine maintains visual displays at a control center. While a spacecraft is being placed in orbit, inputs arrive at the rate of 1000 bits per second. Humans at the control center decide to abort the astronaut if the launch is unsuccessful. Prior to, and for, any abort situation, the machine computes the impact point of the spacecraft. Displays are changed every $\frac{1}{2}$ second during launch, and every 1 second in abort.

In the course of a flight, inputs are transmitted to the computers

---

† The machine configuration for the Mercury Gemini system, described on page 74, differs from the Mercury system discussed here.

from numerous radar tracking stations located around the world. This information must be accepted by the data processing equipment whenever it arrives. The data must then be sorted, edited, and readied for mathematical programs which ascertain and refine the precise orbit of the satellite. Predictions of the spacecraft's position and velocity are transmitted to the tracking stations in advance of its appearance in each area. These data enable radar equipment to pick up the spacecraft before it crosses the station horizon. Information from radar stations is used by the machine to correct its prediction of the path of the astronaut. These calculations enable the computer to compute and display the time to fire the retrorockets to bring the capsule back to earth. During flight, the control center receives new displays of the spacecraft's location, speed, and condition every 6 seconds. Another function performed by the computer is to keep a log of all input data for later analysis.

When the retrorockets are fired for re-entry, the position of the astronaut must be monitored continually, and a prediction made of where he will come down. In the course of this phase, displays are changed every 3 seconds.

To carry out these procedures, a real-time system is needed. The central computer must be able to receive random inputs arriving at varying transmission rates. These entries must be edited simultaneously with the carrying out of mathematical and logical operations. At the same time, the machine must be able to send output messages to a large number of tracking stations and the control center. The computer must maintain numerous different programs with varying priorities in memory, and must have a procedure for deciding when to give control to each program.

REAL-TIME COMMERCIAL APPLICATIONS

Many businesses require a real-time data processing system to provide immediate decisions and to make available fast and accurate service to customers. The American Airlines Sabre system is an application of this type. Here, about 1000 agents, scattered through the United States, are busily engaged in making reservations for customers.

The main problem in a reservation system is to prevent underbooking or overbooking. If there are empty seats on an airplane, potential revenue is lost. On the other hand, if more seats are sold than are available on a flight, extreme customer dissatisfaction may result. The number of seats available on future flights is an airline's inventory. If reservations and cancellations are not reflected immediately in the reservation records, this inventory may not be used with maximum effectiveness. In the absence of a real-time data processing system, agents must make reservations with a less accurate, more cumbersome method in which reservations are made on the basis of availability reports which lag behind actual conditions. In a large operation, under-selling may make a substantial difference in a company's profits.

The magnitude of the American Airlines system is indicated by the anticipated load on the electronic data processing equipment which is being installed. This machinery is daily expected to handle about 40,000 passenger reservations, 30,000 seat availability inquiries, and 20,000 ticket sales, resulting from approximately 85,000 telephone calls. These inputs will pour in from many thousands of miles of linked telephone lines.

The procedure in making a reservation is for the agent to receive a call from a customer, inquiring as to what flights are scheduled for a given day. When the customer selects a particular flight on that date, the agent enters a *need* request to the central processor. If space is available, the machine adjusts the seat inventory for that flight and date. If seats are not open, the computer sends the agent an *availability* display. The same sequence is repeated for the return reservation. Finally, the agent enters the customer's name, address, telephone number, and sundry other items of information into the data processing system.

While the basic method for making a reservation is simple, there are a large number of complex variations on this procedure. For example, the customer may later call up to cancel his reservation, or to change the date or the time of day of certain segments of his itinerary. A large percentage of customers will cancel their reservations, so a wait list must be maintained by the processor. When a seat becomes available for a wait-list customer, the computer must notify his agent, who in turn must telephone the customer to find out if he still wishes to make the reservation. Many itineraries involve interconnections with other airlines, so that procedures must be established to communicate with and make requests from other companies.

The machine system needed for this application must enter into a conversation with the airlines agent at a remote terminal set. Since the agent himself is holding a telephone conversation with a customer, the system is designed to answer 90% of the agent inquiries within 3 seconds to avoid irksome delays in the agent's response to the customer. At peak periods the equipment receives numerous inputs every second. Because of the great complexity of the reservation system, the processor must have available a large number of programs to handle all possible ramifications of customers' requests. Since all of these programs cannot be kept in core memory at the same time, equipment must be maintained for quick access storage, and a programming system devised for bringing in programs when needed. Another requirement is enormous random-access files for storing data. This need is not present in the Mercury computers, but is essential for American Airlines which at times has in the magnitude of 600,000 passenger records in its files. Any one of these reservation records for flights during the next year may be needed at any time by the processor to handle a customer's request. The real-time data processing system for airline reservations must be capable of simultaneously receiving inputs from agents, sending output messages to the remote terminals, receiving and sending teletype messages, executing operational programs, initiating requests for information from disks, drums, or tapes, and receiving data from disks, drums, or tapes.

MULTIPLE-USER COMPUTATIONAL CENTERS

Real-time systems may be used in the future by centralized data processing services. Numerous companies could be tied into a single information-handling center via communication lines from remote terminals. These users would be able to employ the center's computational and processing facilities, as well as large random-access files. The central computer could supply services ranging from mathematical calculation to the recording of individual retail sales and the transmission of output reports to companies' terminals. Ultimately, a number of these on-line service bureaus may spring up in every large city, making data services available on demand to any subscriber.

A start in this direction has been the development of multiconsole computer systems, where a number of programmers can simultaneously compile, debug, or run programs. Such installations reduce the time period between the entry of a program into the system and the time when printed results are available to the user. By enabling programs entered at the consoles to be processed virtually immediately, the value of the computer to engineers and scientists is increased, and the time required for debugging programs is greatly decreased.

To achieve this objective, each user must be able to act as if he had his own, albeit slightly slower, machine. It is necessary, therefore, for the system to be fast enough to avoid keeping the user idle at his console for relatively long periods of time. Long delays would obviously occur if the programs were executed consecutively. Hence some technique such as the round-robin approach, or some variant of this method must be used. In these methods each program, in turn, is allotted a small amount of time on the machine, and this cycling procedure is repeated continually. If the allotted time is in the magnitude of a few seconds, the person at the console can remain in a conversational mode with the computer. Numerous complications arise if all of the programs cannot be kept in core memory simultaneously and if the running programs are permitted to store data on disks.

OTHER APPLICATION AREAS

Real-time data processing is potentially necessary wherever immediate decisions must be made concerning a large, complex, rapidly changing system. For example, whenever customers request credit or management takes action on the basis of current inventory, there is a necessity for a fast analysis of completely current information.

In banking, to cite one possible application, it might be possible to place terminals at each teller's window. These input-output sets would enable every clerk to communicate immediately with ledgers and records stored in a central file. Each teller would enter deposits and withdrawals in his terminal, and the central computer would automatically update the customer's account in a random-access storage. The date and the teller's identification would be included with the posting. The computer would calculate interest and enter it in the file. Record tapes produced at the terminal whenever the tellers entered information would provide an audit trail for every transaction.

Terminals could be located in branches spread over a wide geographical area, and could be connected to the central processor by leased lines. Records might be filed in the IBM 1311 disk storage, which uses removable disks, each storing about 3 million characters of alphanumeric information. Punched-card input-output, a printer, and a console inquiry unit would enable the computer to perform conventional accounting functions when it was not being used by the real-time system. These functions would include the preparation of trial balances, journals, activity listings, and government reports.

Outside of the commercial area there are numerous fields where real-time systems may be used in the future. The employment of teaching machines in classrooms involves a conversational mode between each student and the computer. Problems arise here which are similar to those encountered in multiple-user computational centers.

The library of the future may consist of a central data processor connected to automatic stacks and a group of on-line consoles used by the public for making selections. Records and statistics would be provided by the computer for administrative purposes. The terminals might enable users to interact with the processor in searching a body of literature. Many books, documents, and periodicals could be stored on microfilm, and might be displayed to users by means of viewers at the consoles.

Work has long been under way in the installation of real-time systems in hospitals. The routing of technical instructions and accounting information emanating from doctors' orders involves a large volume of data processing. These procedures could be simplified by making use of terminals linked to a central processor and a random-access storage.

The size and dynamism of modern civilization itself gives rise to many complex states of affairs which often might best be handled by real-time systems. Air traffic control requires continuous monitoring of the positions of all airplanes in the system, and the rapid reshuffling and rescheduling of flights, airlanes, landing places, and queues of planes waiting to land. The optimal routing of automobile traffic in a big city involves similar problems for which communication-based computers have often been suggested.

MILITARY REAL-TIME PROCESSING

Another vast, complex, rapidly changing situation requiring continuous monitoring and immediate decision making is the Sage real-time data processing system. This network of communication-based computers is used for the air defense of the United States. The country is divided into sectors, each of which contains numerous radar stations which maintain continuous surveillance of all aircraft approaching the continent. This information is transmitted immediately to a Sage computer. The computer maintains at all times a complete image of the air situation in its area. This image is based on a continual inflow of data on all air traffic, flight plans, and weather data, and includes the latest information on the disposition of defensive weapons. The computers ascertain the existence and nature of hostile aircraft, determine the optimum assignment of forces available to destroy threatening aircraft, communicate with human command control centers, and produce instructions for the firing and guidance of defensive weapons.

Each sector has available a Bomarc missile which may be located thousands of miles from the computer. These rockets are launched from the ground, and fly at supersonic speeds over a range of about 200 miles. They weigh 15,000 pounds, having a wing span of 18 feet, and can reach an altitude of 70,000 feet. The procedure for firing a Bomarc is as follows:

A radar unit detects an object which might be an approaching airplane, and a small computer on the site calculates its velocity and position. This data is sent to a Sage computer which stores this information for later reference. If shortly thereafter the radar picks up another such object, this data is also transmitted to the central computer. The Sage machine now correlates the two inputs, and decides whether they represent an airplane. If the computer decides that an aircraft is approaching, it evaluates this flight in terms of the air image maintained by the computer. The track of this airplane is displayed visually on a scope for human surveillance. If the aircraft is judged to be hostile, the computer continues to track its course. Humans at the command center decide whether a manned interceptor or a missile will be used to destroy the attacker.

Upon deciding to utilize a Bomarc, a human presses a fire button. The Sage computer immediately transmits prelaunch calculations to the missile, and a second or so later the rocket is fired, entering a vertical climb. The computer now tracks both the enemy airplane and the missile. The course of the Bomarc is corrected continuously by Sage in terms of the position, velocity, and strategy of the hostile airplane. When the rocket is within striking range of the enemy, the Sage computer tips Bomarc into a steep decline and gives control to the missile, which now homes in on the kill.

In this military application there is a need for a real-time data processing system which can simultaneously receive random inputs from many sources, execute a variety of different programs, and send outputs to distant locations. The enormity of this problem is indicated by the fact that, according to one estimate, there are about 125,000 instructions in the Sage system itself, with approximately 15,000 instructions for Bomarc control.

INDUSTRIAL PROCESS CONTROL

Real-time computing systems are of major importance in the automation of certain types of factories and plants. In industrial process control applications a number of rapidly changing variables must be monitored, analyzed, and controlled continuously to produce an optimum result. Industries where computers have been used for real-time control include petroleum refining, steam-electric generating, paper making, and chemicals, cement, and steel manufacturing. It has been estimated that more than 350 real-time process control systems are now in operation, and that as many as 4000 will be installed by 1970.

The speed of electronic data processing machines enables them to make a more rapid, exact response to unanticipated fluctuations in process variables than is possible by human supervision. A computer can readily correlate the behavior of numerous production factors, and integrate the relationships among different variables. Wasteful or dangerous tendencies can be sensed sooner, and instabilities more quickly detected. More precise analysis of operations enables materials and plant equipment to be utilized more efficiently. Quality control is improved, greater safety is achieved, and the cost of maintenance decreased. Computers can also keep a precise, systematic log of all of the processes, thereby providing a better image of overall operating relationships for the planning of future installations.

Real-time data is received by the computer from instruments measuring such variables as temperature, pressure, rate of flow, quality of production, and composition of feed. Inputs to the machine are converted to digital form, and computer outputs for control purposes are transformed, when necessary, into analog information. The computer maintains an image of the overall process, and interrelates its inputs in terms of this representation. The machine adjusts the devices controlling the process continuously so as to maintain optimum performance. Abnormal fluctuations in plant variables can interrupt the currently running program and cause the computer to transfer control to special subroutines for correcting the conditions. A real-time clock included in the processor alerts the machine to scan plant variables at definite intervals, and to initiate control adjustments at appropriate times. The clock also enables the computer to include the time of day when it is logging data. Reports to human supervisors can be printed out on request from the console. These outputs can consist of such information as tables of the values of selected variables, tabulations of computations or inputs, and trend values repeated at predetermined times.

2 THE ENVIRONMENT OF REAL-TIME SYSTEMS

REAL-TIME DATA PROCESSING

In real-time processing, inputs arrive at random from terminals connected to the central processing unit (CPU). The computer rapidly responds to each message, usually by sending an output back to a terminal. This situation is in contrast with conventional *batch processing,* where groups of inputs are processed by passes through the computer.

A real-time system engages in *multiprocessing* when the computer is in conversational interaction with the terminals. From an equipment point of view, multiprocessing occurs when a system contains multiple machine units which share the processing load. *Teleprocessing*† makes use of communication lines. In a real-time application, there is *multiprogramming* if mixing or interleaving of programs occurs.

The notion of *real-time* usually implies that a central processor is responding to inputs within a very short time, perhaps a few seconds. If the duration of time between the creation of information and the computer response is longer, say a matter of hours, most people do not regard the system as "real-time." It is difficult to establish a time criterion to determine whether or not a system is real-time.

I shall not attempt to offer precise definitions of multiprocessing, teleprocessing, multiprogramming, and real-time; nor shall I seek to induce the reader to accept any of the usages I have been describing. What I will do is discuss various systems to which these terms have

† Trademark of IBM.

11

been applied.† Future trends in data processing will probably establish customary terminology.

THROUGHPUT TIME

The main problem in real-time systems is whether the central processing system is fast enough to respond adequately to the messages arriving from the terminals continually. Since inputs enter at random, they may sometimes appear in bunches, sometimes rarely. For several minutes a large number of messages may keep arriving, after which there may be a lull, during which very few, if any, inputs are transmitted to the machine. The frequency distribution of inputs differs obviously for each application. In each instance, a study must be made to ascertain the type of load the system is required to handle.

During periods when inputs are arriving frequently, the computer may not be able to handle each message immediately after its entrance into the machine. When this situation occurs the processor forms a list, or *queue*, of waiting inputs. As each message arrives it is added to the queue. Whenever the machine is ready to process another input, it obtains the next message on the waiting list. Adequate memory must be available to store these inputs, particularly under peak loads, when the number of messages waiting on the queue reaches a maximum. Without sufficient storage for queuing inputs, some of these messages may be lost.

The amount of time a data processing system takes to respond to inputs is called its *throughput* speed. In some applications throughput is largely a function of the speed of the CPU and the size and complexity of the programs needed to process the messages. In cases where files on disks, drums, or tapes must be consulted by the computer, throughput speed is also a function of access time to these peripheral units. Often a machine system may be fast enough to respond adequately to inputs under normal conditions, but may be unable to cope with peak loads. Simulation techniques for evaluating the throughput rates of real-time systems will be discussed in a later chapter.

In some instances it is possible to give the central computer the opportunity to control its volume of input during peak periods. For example, the machine may be able to request inputs only when it is ready. This technique, called *polling*, consists of interrogating the

† This book will not discuss load-sharing in multiple-computer systems.

terminals for information. If the processor becomes too busy, it stops polling for a while.

Another technique may be used if there is a human operator at the other end of the communication line. If the machine is momentarily unable to process an input message, the computer transmits a signal requesting the operator to re-enter his message into the system. Still another method is for the machine simply to send a signal which locks the input device until further notice from the computer.

These techniques can be used only when the terminals can be prevented from originating information, or when the terminals have buffers to hold information until the computer is ready to receive it. In many instances, however, transmission is a matter of urgency: the data originating device has vital information which will be lost if it is not entered immediately. This situation might occur in the case of a pressure gauge in a chemical plant, or a radar station monitoring an air or space flight. The decisive factor is usually how soon the computer must take some action in the situation it is controlling. In a commercial application where the computer is required to respond to remote requests within 3 seconds, it is permissible occasionally for the machine to take longer to respond. Under peak conditions, a relatively long response time may be tolerated depending on the nature of the situation.

THE DATA COMMUNICATION CHANNEL

Even when a machine system is fast enough to perform satisfactorily, it must have the ability to accept inputs with sufficient speed to avoid the loss of information. In Project Mercury, for example, the data communication channel (DCC) provides input-output from an IBM 7090 or 7094 to a variety of devices operating at different transmission rates.

The DCC is attached to the computer in the same manner as a regular data channel. Normally it can include as many as 32 subchannels for handling various types of input-output (I/O) information. The first 10 of these subchannels are set by engineers to be used for high-speed transmission. A sequencer scans the subchannels continually to ascertain whether information is present. When data is ready at a subchannel, the sequencer stops and requests a memory storage cycle from the CPU. Information is placed in core storage in eight-bit fashion when a storage cycle is available. None of the arithmetic or logical registers are affected. The sequencer remains at a subchannel until the storage cycle is granted and the data are transferred into the main frame memory. The amount of time the sequencer remains at a subchannel depends on the particular instruction then being executed by the CPU. This determines when the next memory cycle will be available. The high-speed subchannels are given priority by the sequencer. Before it steps to the next position in the scan, the sequencer ascertains whether any of the first 10 subchannels are ready to request a memory cycle.

Each subchannel is assigned a block of core as a buffer. The particular area of memory allocated is reserved through switches set by the engineers. Each subchannel has a counter associated with its available core locations. The counter is stepped each time the subchannel places a word in the buffer. When the entire buffer area has been filled, or when an *end-of-message* character is received by the subchannel, an *interrupt* or *trap* is executed by the hardware. This consists of placing certain control information in memory location 00003, and transferring program control to location 00004.

After a trap has occurred, all further interrupts from other subchannels are inhibited. Location 00004 gives control to an interrupt subroutine which performs certain necessary functions. If further traps were permitted while this subroutine was being executed, this subroutine could itself be interrupted, and a chaotic situation could result. An *enabling* instruction is available which can remove the inhibition. This enable is placed at the end of the interrupt subroutine, thereby once more permitting traps to occur.

Although additional interrupts are inhibited after the first trap, a second interrupt is remembered. If a second interrupt request occurs, the sequencer stops at this subchannel and no data is sent to memory. If a second interrupt request does not occur during the inhibition period, the high-speed subchannels are permitted to obtain storage cycles to place more words in their buffers. If this were not permitted, the DCC would not be able to operate under high loads, because inputs entering in close succession to one another could not be handled.

INTERRUPT SUBROUTINES

The interrupt subroutine must be able to carry out all of its functions fast enough to avoid losing new information coming in on the subchannels. For a 32K machine, the control information placed automatically in location 00003 at the time of an interrupt consists of a 36-bit word containing the following information:

Bit position	Control information
S (sign bit)	End-of-message signal received prior to the counter reaching this position. This is an error condition.
1	Interrupt caused by the DCC, rather than by some other I/O device connected to the system.
2, 3	Which DCC caused the interrupt. (There may be more than one DCC connected to the system.)
4–8	Which subchannel caused the interrupt.
21–35	The contents of the instruction counter when the interrupt occurred.

The main function of the interrupt subroutine is to move the input information out of the memory buffer into another part of memory where a queue of inputs from this subchannel is maintained. To perform this task, the interrupt subroutine, which is used for all subchannels, must know which subchannel caused the interrupt. This information is contained in the control word at 00003. Upon ascertaining which subchannel caused the trap, the interrupt subroutine knows which buffer to operate upon. A final task of the interrupt subroutine, after enabling further traps, is to transfer control back to the program which was running when the interrupt took place. This is made possible by the presence of the former contents of the instruction counter in the control word. This information permits the interrupt subroutine to return control to the proper instruction in the interrupted program. Of course, the first action of the interrupt subroutine is to save the contents of certain machine registers used by the trapped program; one of its last actions is to restore these registers. The registers which are saved are those which the subroutine itself uses, and whose contents it would destroy while its instructions were being executed.

It is necessary for the interrupt subroutine to be fast enough to clear the buffer area before the subchannel associated with that buffer obtains more data to be moved into that part of memory. If this is not done, the information in the buffer is read over by the new messages, and is thereby lost. Another problem is that, while the machine is handling an interrupt, new information coming in on other subchannels may have no place to be stored. It is necessary in planning a machine system to determine in advance what the worst combination of inputs could be, and then to ascertain whether the interrupt subroutine is fast enough to handle this worst case. In the Mercury system the interrupt subroutines all run in the order of 1 millisecond, a time sufficiently small for any contingency. In some applications it is not necessary for the machine to be able to handle the worst possible case, for redundancy among the inputs may enable the computer to make all required calculations even if some of the input data are lost.

The task of the interrupt subroutine is made easier if subchannels are not assigned fixed locations in core as buffers, and if commands can be stored in the channel. With this method, the interrupt subroutine has merely to provide the channel with the address of the next available block of storage which can be utilized as a buffer. The subroutine does not have to move the information to another part of memory.

TERMINAL SETS

In a commercial real-time system, transactions originate at terminal sets, where they are entered by employees or agents. Messages sent from the terminals pass through a communication network to the central processor. The computer responds by transmitting information back to the remote terminal in such forms as a typewritten message, a lighting of indicators, or as output punched into a paper tape. Transactions may be initiated by telegraph sets as well as by terminals.

The agents' sets used in the airlines applications include a unit for the machine reading of an air information sheet. Each agent has a file of these sheets which are analogous to punched cards. Each sheet lists a number of flights between two cities, and contains holes which can be sensed by the agents' sets. When an agent needs information on a particular flight, he selects from his file the sheet which lists this flight. He places the sheet in a holder which enables the terminal to sense the data. Buttons on the set enable the agent to select any particular flight on the sheet. Other keys permit the agent to enter information on routine matters such as the date and number of seats requested. Inputs of a nonroutine nature are placed in the system by a typewriter which also prints output messages from the main computer. Availability lights on the set are activated by the central processor when flight seats requested by the agent are open.

In the Sabre system, data from communication lines are assembled into 36-bit words in a real-time channel, and from there are moved into the core storage of the main processor. This channel is able to handle 16 input lines and 16 output lines. The flow of data on each line is under the control of commands placed in the real-time channel by the computer. Thirty-two programs are kept in the memory of the processor, each of which controls one of the input-output lines.

TERMINAL INTERCHANGES

The lines from the central computer, also called *trunks,* can be connected with as many as 30 *terminal interchanges.* These inter-changes are units which collect messages from the terminals, provide buffering, and transmit information to the processor at the rate of 2000 bits per second. The terminal interchanges perform similar functions for output messages from the data processing center to the agents' sets.

Each terminal interchange contains a 4000 character storage. This consists of 39 100-character buffers, and a 100-character section for control information. A message from an agent's set is accumulated in one 100-character buffer. If an agent makes a mistake, he can clear a buffer by pressing a *reset* button. Up to 98 characters can be assembled in one buffer; two other characters, the terminal address character and the end-of-message character, are added automatically. When 98 characters from an agent's set have accumulated in one buffer, or when an end-of-message character is sensed, the message is ready to be transmitted to the main computer.

Buffers are not associated permanently with a particular agent's set, but are assigned on demand to these terminals. Messages in excess of 98 characters are automatically allocated another 100-character buffer after the first buffer has been filled. Additional segments of such long messages are confined to 97 characters each—one character is needed to identify the next buffer load as a continuation of the previous segment.

Messages from the central processor to the agents' sets are restricted to 100 characters, including the terminal address character and the end-of-message character. Where output messages consist of more than 100 characters, the computer treats all characters in excess of 98 as separate messages.

The terminal interchange forms a control word for each message it processes. These control words are stored in its memory, and are brought out into a control register when needed. Here are some of the functions performed by the control words:

(a) Assign a buffer to each input or output message, and update the storage position of the character being processed.

(b) Control an output message until a terminal set is ready to receive it.

(c) Ready queue messages for transmission to the central processor.

(d) Perform a parity check on characters received from the terminals.

OPERATIONS OF TERMINAL INTERCHANGES

The following are simplified descriptions of how the terminal interchange processes information:

(a) *Input from agent's set to interchange:* Each character sent from an agent's set to a terminal interchange consists of nine bits. These bits, sent serially, consist of a start bit, a check bit, six data bits, and a stop bit. As the bits arrive they are placed in a data register, which is continually shifted to make room for incoming bits. When the stop bit arrives, the start bit is at the other end of the register, where it is sensed; this initiates the transmission of the character from the data register into the assigned buffer storage region. The characters are gradually assembled in the buffer. The buffer is assigned and its location placed in a control word when the message begins. The message from the agent's set is placed in the proper buffer position under the direction of the control word.

(b) *Transmission from interchange to computer:* When a buffer is filled or an end-of-message character is sensed, that buffer load is placed on a queue of messages to be sent to the central processor. A queue counter is increased by one whenever a message is placed in this queue.

Whenever the computer is ready to receive input messages, it sends a go-ahead signal to the most remote terminal interchange on each of its communication lines. Now each of these most remote terminal interchanges sends all of the messages which have accumulated in its buffers since the terminal's last transmission period. After each message is sent to the processor the queue counter is decreased by one. When the queue counter reaches zero, that interchange sends a go-ahead signal to the next terminal interchange. The *next* interchange is that unit on the line which is now the most remote terminal interchange from the central computer. This interchange transmits all of its messages, and then sends a go-ahead to the next most remote interchange.

This process is continued until all interchanges have sent in their messages. After the closest terminal interchange has finished transmitting its information, it sends a signal to the central computer, which then initiates another cycle by sending a go-ahead signal to the most remote interchange.

(c) *Transmission from processor to interchange:* When the central computer commences to transmit a message, a buffer is assigned to this message, and its address is placed in a control word. The output characters from the processor are placed in the proper positions in the buffer, under the direction of the control word. The terminal interchange calculates a check character based on each data character it receives. After the entire message has been received, the interchange compares its check character with a check character sent by the computer at the end of the message. If the message is correct, control is given to a control word responsible for directing the transmission of the message to the proper agent's set. The terminal interchange is now ready to receive another output from the processor.

(d) *Transmission from interchange to agents' sets:* Output to an agent's set occurs immediately if the set is free. If the agent's set is busy, the message is placed in waiting status, and is transmitted as soon as the set is able to receive the information.

The terminal interchange can operate in only one of the above four processing modes at a time. However, the input and output of information is interleaved and is so rapid that for practical purposes all inputs and outputs can be regarded as being handled simultaneously.

An input communication adapter and output communication adapter enable data to be transmitted between telegraph devices and the IBM data processing equipment. These adapters are necessary

because telegraphic and IBM equipment both use different codes, operate at different speeds, and employ unlike controls.

THE MINIMIZATION OF COMMUNICATION NETWORKS

The cost of a transmission system is to a large extent a function of
the loads carried by the network and the number of miles over which
the messages are transmitted. Where a central computer is linked to a
number of geographically distant terminals, the problem of designing

City	Load
New York, N. Y.	13250
Syracuse, N. Y.	545
Buffalo, N. Y.	1135
Philadelphia, Penn.	1475
Pittsburgh, Penn.	830
Washington, D. C.	1465
Lynchburg, Va.	755
Charleston, W. Va.	380
New Bern, N. C.	1205
Charlotte, N. C.	670
Atlanta, Ga.	1210
Jacksonville, Fla.	1385
Daytona Beach, Fla.	1290
Orlando, Fla.	1750
Tampa, Fla.	1115
Miami, Fla.	2540
Key West, Fla.	780
Detroit, Mich.	1685
Milwaukee, Wisc.	930
Madison, Wisc.	495
St. Paul, Minn.	970
Minneapolis, Minn.	1060
Duluth, Minn.	455
Chicago, Ill.	6935
Effingham, Ill.	230
South Bend, Ill.	2440
Ft. Wayne, Ind.	710
Anderson, Ind.	1315
Indianapolis, Ind.	3620
Evansville, Ind.	815
Lima, Ohio	465
Nashville, Tenn.	585
St. Louis, Mo.	2140

a minimum-cost communication network becomes economically significant. The planning of transmission lines is a large undertaking in systems engineering, and deserves several chapters for adequate treatment. Included here is an example of such problems. In this particular case, it was possible to work out a mathematical technique for minimizing the communication network.

This one situation consisted of 33 cities spread over the east coast of the United States. A condition of the problem was that the total traffic on a given transmission line could not exceed 90% of that line's capacity. Above is a list of the cities involved in the hookup. The load from each city terminal is stated in terms of the number of characters sent in the peak 15 minutes.

The traffic rates for 600-character-per-minute teletype lines, used from 9 A.M. to 5 P.M., 5 days a week, are as follows:

Distance	Rate
0–250 miles	$1.12 per mile per month
250–500 miles	$280 + $1.01 per mile per month
500–1000 miles	$533 + $0.90 per mile per month
1000–1500 miles	$983 + $0.79 per mile per month
1500 and over	$1378 + $0.67 per mile per month

The design problem involves finding a way of connecting all of these cities so as to minimize the transmission costs. This problem has certain affinities to the mathematical theory of trees.

A mathematical tree is a type of graph in which each pair of terminals is connected by only one line. For example, the diagram shown in Fig. 2-1 contains 125 possible trees. Six of these are shown in Fig. 2-2.

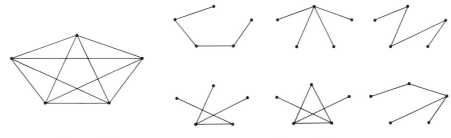

FIGURE 2-1   FIGURE 2-2

FIGURE 2-3

A network of 33 cities contains a billion, trillion, trillion different possible trees. Obviously no computer, much less a human designer, can examine all of these possibilities. However, the use of the mathematical theory of trees permits a minimum cost network to be devised without an exhaustive search. Figure 2-3 shows the minimal communication configuration for the 33 cities which was obtained by a 7090 computer in 30 minutes by using the tree technique:

3 MULTIPROGRAMMING FOR REAL-TIME SYSTEMS

OVERLAPPING OF INPUT-OUTPUT WITH INTERNAL PROCESSING

In early tape processing machines, the CPU was often idle while awaiting the completion of input-output (I/O) operations. Many of the first computers were unable to proceed with further instructions until the completion of a previous read or write order. Hence, there was a long delay while the tape reels began to turn and while a length of tape moved past the read-write head. Since many problems required extensive input or output, the CPU was often not utilized a large percentage of the time.

One of the first attempts to reduce this inefficiency consisted of introducing tape buffers. An input buffer is essentially a high-speed storage unit which temporarily holds information read from tape. Whenever a running program is ready for more data, it gives an instruction which dumps the contents of the buffer into main memory and initiates the refilling of the buffer from the tape unit. While the CPU is processing the new buffer load, the buffer is receiving another load from tape. This arrangement provides overlapping of CPU time with tape time. Such overlapping is obviously possible with both input and output buffers.

Here is a simple illustration of the value of buffering. Assume that a problem consists of reading and processing records. The time to read a record from tape is 10 milliseconds, and the time to process each record is 5 milliseconds.

Unbuffered Input

	0	10	15	25	30	40	45	55
CPU time	10 ms idle	5 ms process	10 ms idle	5 ms process	10 ms idle	5 ms process	10 ms idle	
Input tape time	10 ms input	5 ms idle	10 ms input	5 ms idle	10 ms input	5 ms idle	10 ms input	
	0	10	15	25	30	40	45	55

Buffered Input

		Dump buffer		Dump buffer		Dump buffer		Dump buffer		Dump buffer		Dump buffer
	0		15		25		35		45		55	
CPU time	10 ms idle	5 ms process	5 ms idle	5 ms process	5 ms idle	5 ms process	5 ms idle	5 ms process	5 ms idle	5 ms process	5 ms idle
Input tape time	10 ms input	10 ms input		10 ms input		10 ms input		10 ms input		10 ms input	
	0	10	20		30		40		50		60	

In the unbuffered case the CPU is busy $33\frac{1}{3}\%$ of the time, and the tape unit is occupied $66\frac{2}{3}\%$ of the time. With buffering, the CPU is 50% busy after the initial read-in, and the tape is utilized 100% of the time.

DATA CHANNELS

The use of data channels was another step forward. The data channel contains a 36-bit buffer, along with control circuits for storing and executing commands. Commands are sent to the channel by CPU instructions, and are executed independently of the CPU. Whenever the buffer is filled, the channel automatically seizes the next memory cycle from the CPU program, and uses this time to store the buffer's data in memory. This process does not disturb the CPU registers.

If the instruction under way in the CPU is not using main memory, the data from the channel enter into memory simultaneously with the execution of the instruction. In this case no CPU time is lost. If the CPU instruction requires memory access when the channel seizes a memory cycle, the instruction must wait one cycle. Where a computer has multiple data channels, two or more requests for memory cycles may occur simultaneously. The machine automatically establishes memory-access priorities in such contingencies.

The data channel thus not only provides for overlapping of CPU and tape time; but in many instances overlaps the entry of channel data with CPU instruction execution. This technique also frees the

CPU from the task of controlling the flow of input data; autonomous channel commands bring information into the machine and place it in the assigned memory locations.

TRAPPING

A channel must be able to signal the CPU at the end of input operations, when reaching end of file, or upon a redundancy tape check. Communication from channel to CPU occurs by trapping (interrupting). By interrupting a normal CPU instruction sequence, a trap alerts the CPU to a special condition requiring immediate attention. For example, an interrupt at the completion of an input tape operation notifies the CPU program that it can now make use of this input data and may now command the channel to commence other tape operations. The alternative to trapping would be a periodic interrogation of a trigger to ascertain the completion of the tape input.

When a trap takes place, the CPU completes its current instruction and stores the contents of the instruction counter (IC) in a special memory location. The CPU obtains its next instruction from another specified word in core. When channel A traps, the IBM 7090 stores IC in location 0012, and gets the next instruction from 0013. The transfer of control gives the CPU the opportunity to enter a program to perform certain required activities. We are denoting such programs as *trap subroutines* or *interrupt subroutines*. The storage of IC provides a way for these routines to return to the next instruction in the trapped program.

As we have seen, one of the first actions taken by an interrupt subroutine is to prevent itself from destroying needed information in the CPU registers used by the trapped program. To save this data, the interrupt subroutine stores the contents of the registers employed by itself. When the subroutine ends, it restores these registers prior to returning control to the trapped program.

The instruction set contains a method for *enabling* or *disabling* traps. Disabling is necessary when it is undesirable to interrupt a sequence of instructions. We have noted that when a trap occurs the computer automatically inhibits additional interrupts. This prevents a later trap from interrupting a trap subroutine. Enabling permits traps to occur after inhibition or disabling has taken place. The instruction causing an enable is placed at the very end of an interrupt subroutine. However, it is not immediately executed. The next instruction—an unconditional transfer of control—is executed before enabling becomes effective. Otherwise a trap could occur before the interrupt subroutine gave control back to the original program.

MULTIPROGRAMMING

Even with data channels, in many programs the CPU stalls while an I/O operation is under way. The problem of unused CPU time is intensified when the machine system includes disk units. Here access time is between 50-180 milliseconds. The CPU may be idle for long periods of time while a program awaits data from a disk.

One solution to this problem is to keep two programs in memory at the same time. Whenever the first program stalls, control is transferred to the second program. The CPU works on the second program while the first program's I/O is under way. As soon as the first program's I/O is complete it can use the CPU again. This procedure is satisfactory so long as the second program itself does not require input-output, in which case both programs may stall while waiting for I/O completions. A way out of this difficulty is to keep several programs in memory simultaneously. The more programs in memory, the greater is the possibility of having a program available which can use the CPU when the other programs are stalled. Whenever such a program is available, the CPU can keep busy.

The amount of core storage limits the number of programs which may remain in memory at the same time. After a certain point there is no space for additional programs. Accordingly, the efficiency of multiprogramming depends upon the size of the programs, as well as the frequency and duration of their I/O requests. Infrequent I/O operations and low access times for completing I/O requests alleviate the necessity of finding another program to keep the CPU busy. The general problem of keeping all of the facilities in a machine system as busy as possible is called *multiprogram scheduling*. (See discussion on page 164.)

CONTROL PROGRAMS†

In a multiprogrammed system, a special *control program* remains in memory at all times. Two of its main purposes are to handle I/O

---

† Various types of control systems have been devised for differing systems' needs. It should be noted here that many real-time systems do not use multiprogramming. Sabre-type applications are much more complex than many real-time systems.

requests and to keep track of programs needing the CPU. The control program is supervisory in nature, as compared with the *operational* programs which actually process data or solve problems. Among the many other functions of the control program are storage allocation and the reading-in of operational programs as needed.†

Operational programs communicate with the control program by using macros (macro instructions), into which the operational programs place whatever information is needed by the control program. Macros call upon subroutines within the control program. As we shall see, a large number of system functions are carried out by the various macro instructions.

Operational programs cannot be permitted to initiate I/O operations, and, therefore, must request input or output by means of macros. This enables the control program to give control of the CPU to another operational program. Without this requirement, an operational program might request access to an external storage unit while that unit was already in use as the result of a previous request by another operational program. If the second operational program were allowed to give I/O instructions, the CPU would be stalled until the prior I/O operation was complete. Hence, the second operational program must make its requests through the control program.

By means of macros, operational programs yield control to the control program, supplying it with all of the information needed to initiate a requested input or output operation. Upon receiving control, the control program ascertains whether a previous request for the same I/O unit is still under way; if so, the control program places the new request in a waiting list. If no previous request for the I/O unit is currently being executed, the control program initiates the new request.

After either initiating the new request or placing it in a queue, the control program gives control of the CPU to another operational program. If there are a number of operational programs in the machine, the availability status of each program is kept in a list called the *CPU queue*. When a program terminates or awaits the completion of an I/O request, it is removed from this queue. The control program refers to this list when it wishes to give control of the CPU to another operational program. In some applications, certain operational programs may have priority for receiving control before other programs in the queue.

Whenever an I/O operation is complete, the running operational

† The Sabre control program consists of about 6000 instructions. The operational programs are composed of approximately 150,000 instructions.

program is interrupted, and control goes to the control program. A subroutine records the fact that the operational program which made this request is once more ready to use the CPU. This is done by entering this program into the CPU queue. The interrupt subroutine now looks in the list of I/O requests. If any items are in this queue, it initiates the next request. The control program now returns control to the interrupted operational program. Since the contents of the instruction counter were stored automatically when the trap occurred, the control program utilizes this address for returning control to the next instruction in the interrupted operational program.

THE CPU LOOP

The efficiency of batch processing can be increased by keeping more than one program in memory, and by overlapping I/O requests with CPU usage. In real-time situations each input message, or *entry*, must be processed by an operational program. In a commercial system, most operational programs require a disk or drum access, after which an output is sent back to the terminal. Because of the large volume of entries, several messages are usually in the central computer waiting to be processed. Since handling most entries involves an I/O request delay, it is necessary to use multiprogramming to avoid intolerable delays in responding to inputs.†

The arrival of an entry causes a trap to an interrupt subroutine in the control program. This subroutine places the entry into the real-time queue. Whenever CPU time becomes available because of an operational program's I/O request, the control program can consult the real-time queue to find an operational program to use CPU time. There are thus two lists of available operational programs: the real-time queue and the CPU queue.

In addition to these queues, a system usually has certain programs which must run at definite time intervals. A real-time clock is employed for this purpose. It is either set to interrupt at specified times, or else is frequently interrogated by the control program. A *time-activated* queue is maintained, and is consulted by the control program when CPU time is available.

A fourth category of available programs consists of batch-type

---

† Where the overhead of control program bookkeeping outweighs the advantage of multiprogramming, this technique is, of course, not used.

programs which are kept on a standby basis, to be run in case the CPU has idle time.

The core of the control program, a routine called the *CPU loop,* receives control whenever an operational program is stalled awaiting the completion of an I/O request. The CPU queue may be examined before the real-time queue, or vice-versa. However, in essence, the CPU loop program functions as shown in Fig. 3-1.

In actuality, the CPU loop program is somewhat more complicated than the diagram below indicates. A real-time system must be kept in continual operation, since it is at the heart of a dynamically changing situation. It is crucial for the central computer to respond within a small number of seconds. In some instances an excessive delay may be catastrophic. Therefore, a second, backup machine is often included in the system. If the first machine is malfunctioning, control is given to the duplex computer.

For a similar reason, halt instructions are not permissible in real-time systems. The time required by a console operator to notice that the machine has stopped, to decide what to do next, and to transfer control manually to an appropriate location, would delay the system significantly. Although halt instructions can be eliminated when programs are compiled, a halt order can be generated by machine error, or through mistakes in programming. Another similar possibility is the creation of an endless loop in one of the running programs.

An alarm clock within the computer recognizes such conditions. Its time period is usually set in the magnitude of 100 milliseconds. If the clock is not reset before the expiration of this interval, a signal is produced which initiates manual or automatic switchover to the duplex computer. One of the functions of the CPU loop is to reset the alarm. The clock interval is set to exceed substantially the duration of any operational program. Since the CPU loop routine receives control after the termination or partial completion of operational programs, it is always able to reset the timer before a clock period elapses. Normally, the alarm is reset long before the interval expires.

Another complication in the CPU loop program arises from the fact that it is very frequently executed. For system efficiency, this program should run enabled: it must be possible for traps to occur during the CPU loop. If the CPU loop ran in the disabled state, the real-time communication lines could never trap during these frequent intervals. Under certain conditions this might result in the loss of real-time mes-

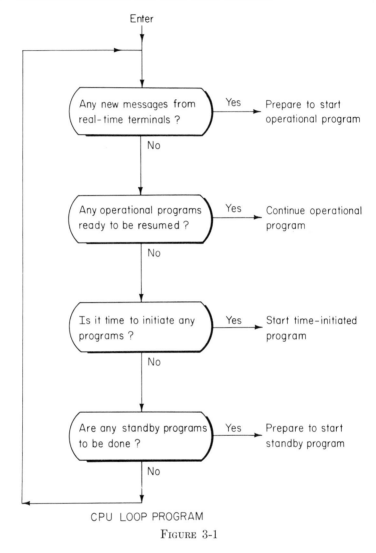

CPU LOOP PROGRAM

FIGURE 3-1

sages. It is also valuable to enable disk channel traps during the CPU loop. This permits new commands to be sent to channels immediately after the completion of I/O operations. If channel traps were disabled, the channels would frequently be idle for short intervals of time, thereby decreasing the response time of the system.

However, a programming difficulty could arise if the CPU loop program ran enabled. This problem would occur if a real-time trap subroutine or channel trap subroutine attempted to add a new item

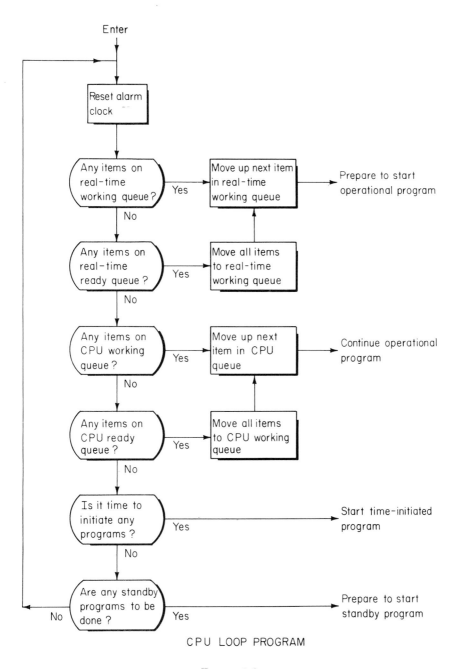

CPU LOOP PROGRAM

FIGURE 3-2

to the real-time queue or CPU queue just as the interrupted CPU loop program was about to remove an item from one of these queues. To avoid this difficulty, each of the queues is broken into two parts: *ready* and *working*. Hence, there is established a real-time ready queue and a real-time working queue, as well as a CPU ready queue and a CPU working queue. New items are always added to the ready queue, whereas items to be used are taken from the working queue. The CPU loop program first examines the working queue; if an item is present in this queue, it transfers control to that item's operational program. If no items are present in the working queue, the CPU loop examines the ready queue. If items exist in the ready queue, the CPU loop program moves all of them to the working queue, after which it transfers control to the next operational program.

With these complexities added, the CPU loop program appears as shown in Fig. 3-2.

4 REAL-TIME STORAGE ALLOCATION

ALLOCATION OF STORAGE

The contents of core storage in a real-time data processing system are volatile and unpredictable. It is not possible to know in advance how many input messages will be in memory at a given time, since these inputs are continually arriving at random, being serviced, and terminated. In the American Airlines system, an *entry block* of about 78 words, or 468 characters, is made available for each message. The entry block remains in core during the entire period from arrival of the input to the completion of its processing. It thus provides storage for the original message and its associated information during intervals when the entry's operational program is stalled waiting for the completion of an I/O request, or is on a CPU queue waiting to be resumed. Certain control information is also stored in the entry block.

In addition to the entry block, some messages require for their processing other working storage areas in memory. This additional storage is available in standard blocks of the same size as the entry block. Blocks of 256 words are employed for segments of the operational program(s) used for the processing of each message.

The number of blocks needed for program and data storage fluctuates continually in an unforeseeable way. Furthermore, it is impossible to foretell which of the messages in core at a given time will be completed first. Response time for each entry depends on numerous variable factors, such as length of its operational program, number of I/O requests required, and access time to complete these I/O requests. Since there is no way to determine beforehand what portions of core storage will be in use at a particular time, it is not practical to assign core storage, as needed, by any type of sequential allotment of available memory. If this method were attempted, "holes" of available storage would continually form. The filling and utilization of these gaps would require extensive, time-consuming bookkeeping.

LIST STRUCTURES

At American Airlines, *list structures* are used for allocating storage. A list structure consists of a set of fixed-size blocks of storage which are "chained" together. The first word in each block, called a *pointer* word, contains the core address of the next block in the chain; the remainder of each block contains data. Starting at the first word in a list, it is easily possible to sequence through the entire chain by using the address in the pointer word of each block. The blocks belonging in the list may be scattered anywhere throughout memory, but as members of the list, they are parts of an organized structure which can be manipulated easily and rapidly by list programs.

A base word at a fixed location in core storage contains the address of the first block in the list. The last block in the list is designated by

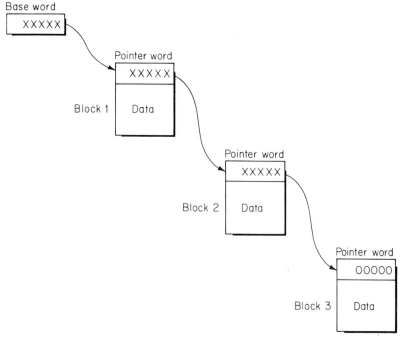

FIGURE 4-1

some special symbol, such as zeros, in its pointer word. A three-block list takes the form shown in Fig. 4-1.

Figure 4-2 is an example of how a four-block list structure actually might appear in core storage.

The base word, in location 0100, points to the first block in the list, whose absolute address is 0109. The pointer word of the first block contains 0105, the address of the second block in the list. The final member of the list, block four, is reached by following from each pointer word to the next. The pointer word of block four contains the terminating symbol, 0000.

To add a block to the end of a list, a subroutine replaces the zero in the pointer word of the last block by the address of the new block. A zero is then placed in the pointer word of the new block, which is now the last block in the list.

To delete the first block in a list, a subroutine replaces the address in the base word by the address in the pointer word of the first block.

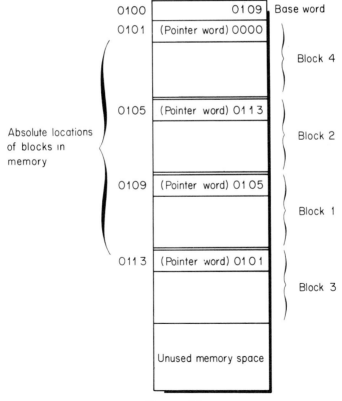

FIGURE 4-2

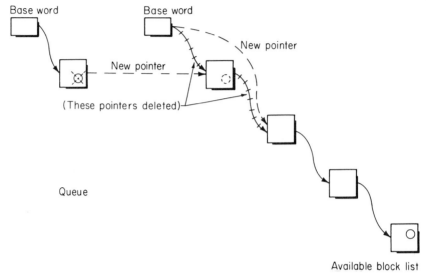

Adding a new block to a queue
from an available block list (dotted lines indicate this action)

FIGURE 4-3

The new address in the base word now points to the block which was formerly second in the list.

Several subroutines, called *list operators,* are used to manipulate list structures. Various list languages, such as Professor John McCarthy's LISP and Newell and Simon's IPL, have been developed for "artificial intelligence" purposes. However, for the relatively simple needs of storage allocation in real-time systems, a small number of list subroutines are sufficient.

When a new block is added to a list, where does the subroutine find an available unused block? Since a list may be scattered randomly throughout core storage, it would be time consuming to search memory every time a new block is needed. To avoid such searches, an *available block list* is maintained. This list contains all unused blocks. If a new block is needed, the first (or last) block is deleted from the available block list, and added to the beginning (or end) of the other list. When the system is first started, the available block list is initialized to contain all possible blocks. As blocks are needed for other lists, they are obtained from the available block list. When blocks on lists are no longer needed, they are deleted and returned to the available block list. The available list is initially given enough blocks to provide for the maximum needs of the system. Every block provided for in memory is always a member of some list.

Queues are usually maintained in the form of list structures. Figure 4-3 shows an example of a block being added to a queue from an available list.

There is no physical movement of blocks in list operations. All that occurs is the movement of pointers from one pointer word to another. The use of index registers or indirect addressing in the coding facilitates this shifting around of pointers. In terms of absolute core locations, the above addition of a new block to a queue from an available block list might appear as shown in Fig. 4-4.

The CPU work list uses a first-in, first-out procedure. The next

Adding a new block to a queue
from an available block list

	Before		After
2000	2016 — 2nd block in available block list	2000	2016 — 1st block in available block list
2004	0000 — 4th and last block in available block list	2004	0000 — 3rd and final block in available block list
2008	0000 — 1st and only block in queue	2008	2012 — 1st block in queue
2012	2000 — 1st block in available block list	2012	0000 — 2nd block in queue
2016	2004 — 3rd block in available block list	2016	2004 — 2nd block in available block list
2020	2008 Base word for queue	2020	2008 Base word for queue
2021	2012 Base word for available block list	2021	2000 Base word for available block list

FIGURE 4-4

program to be resumed is the program which has been waiting for the longest time. Hence, blocks are always added to the top of the list, and removed from the bottom. To perform this operation, the base word contains not only the address of the first block in the list, but also the address of the last block in the list.

In a push-down list, items are added to the top of the list and removed from the top of the list. This type of list can be utilized for a last-in, first-out operation such as may be useful in the available block list. In some instances it is useful for the list to contain back references; then each pointer word contains not only the address of the next block in the chain, but also the address of its predecessor block.

MEMORY PROTECTION

In a multiprogrammed system, a number of operational programs are usually in core storage at the same time. In addition, memory contains various queues and the control program, which itself is comprised of numerous subroutines and tables. In such a system, it is possible for an operational program to address portions of memory outside of its own coding, data areas, working storages, and constants. This problem could result from either a programming or machine error. As a consequence, modification of instructions or alteration of data in another operational program might occur. Another effect could be impairment of the control program. Improper tape, disk, or drum operations might be initiated, and crucial records could be affected. A further possibility is the formation of endless loops or halts. If more than one customer employed the system, it would be possible for users to have access to each other's private information.

To avoid such possibilities, some form of memory protection may be regarded as desirable. Obviously, it would be intolerably time consuming for the control program to monitor all instructions in operational programs. Moreover, any method of establishing limits on the memory references made by operational programs would have to take into account that these limits would be changing continually, owing to the volatile allocation of core storage. In addition, different limits would have to be set around each operational program.

A technique employed at the Massachusetts Institute of Technology relies on additional equipment, in the form of a lower boundary register and an upper boundary register. Special instructions set these registers, and place the CPU in the protection mode. While in this mode, the machine compares every instruction about to be executed with the boundary registers. If the address part of an instruction is outside of these limits, the instruction is not executed. Instead, a trap occurs, causing the storage of the instruction counter into a fixed location and a transfer of control to a specified word in core. This interrupt causes the CPU to leave the protection mode, thereby permitting a subroutine to intervene.

Instructions which contain transfers are not trapped by the boundary registers. However, the address in the instruction counter is compared to the boundary registers during *I-time* (cycles when instructions are fetched from core and interpreted). Hence, an improper transfer instruction will be trapped in the I-cycle following its execution. A special indicator enables the control program to ascertain what has occurred.

Both of the boundary registers are set with one instruction. The machine does not enter the protection mode, however, until one additional instruction has been executed. This gives the control program the opportunity to transfer to an operational program after setting the boundary registers. Otherwise, this transfer instruction would itself be trapped.

Since an operational program cannot be permitted to alter its own limits, the instruction setting the boundary registers is itself trapped if the CPU is in the protection mode. All I/O instructions also cause interrupts during this mode.

PROGRAM RELOCATION

In a large system, core is not large enough to hold all operational programs simultaneously. Since messages enter at random, it is not possible to plan which operational programs (other than those used frequently) should be kept permanently in core. At any given time, a number of programs will be in memory, in various stages of completion. In American Airlines, whenever another operational program is needed, it is allotted a block from the available block list prior to being read into core. Operational programs must be prepared in block-size segments.

Since a segment of an operational program may be placed anywhere in core storage, all instructions must be modified for proper execution of the program. This modification, or program relocation, can occur either when a program is read into memory, or immediately before the execution of each instruction.

The former technique is similar to the loading of relocatable programs in conventional computer installations. The problem is to ascertain which instructions must have their addresses modified, and which may be left unchanged. It would be an error to modify the address part of instructions such as *shift* orders. However, it would be too laborious for a loader to examine each operation code to determine the necessity of address modification. Therefore, a relocatable loader uses an indicator in the form of a hole in a punched card, which is associated with each instruction during compilation. This bit indicates to the loader whether or not it should modify the associated address. In a multiprogrammed system, an analogous procedure can be followed by employing a small amount of additional equipment. In American Airlines, the *tag* field of each instruction contains two or more bits when modification of the address portion during loading is required. (The "tag" is a three-bit field used to specify which index registers are to be used when an instruction is executed.) The tag is set for address modification during loading by a special routine in the compiler. This method places a minor restriction on programmers' use of multiple index registers.

The technique of modifying addresses at execution time is used at M.I.T. A specially installed relocation register behaves like an index register, incrementing any address employed in making a memory reference. Instructions such as shifts are not affected since they do not involve access to memory. To modify transfer-type orders (which do not make memory reference), the address in the instruction counter is incremented during the I-cycle. In this way the address used to fetch the next instruction from storage is properly incremented. Special instructions load and store the relocation register.

The following example shows a program compiled for locations 1000 . . . 1003, which is allocated locations 5000 . . . 5003. (The instruction CLA clears the accumulator, and adds the contents of the designated memory location into the accumulator. TRA is an unconditional transfer of control. STO stores the contents of the accumulator in the designated memory location.)

					During execution	
					Effective	Effective
Compiled for			Allocated to		IC	address
1000	CLA	1100	5000	CLA	1100	5000	5100
1001	TRA	1003	5001	TRA	1003	5001	1003
1002	STO	1101	5002	STO	1101	....	....
1003	ADD	1102	5003	ADD	1102	5003	5102

The control program places the number 4000 in the relocation register, enters relocation mode, then transfers control to location 1000. The number now in IC, namely 1000, is incremented by 4000, thereby causing the instruction in 5000 to be fetched. This instruction, CLA 1100, is also incremented by 4000, thus addressing the operand in 5100. The TRA 1003 instruction, executed without modification, places 1003 in IC. However, during the next I-cycle, this 1003 is increased by 4000, and the instruction in 5003 is obtained.

The machine does not actually enter the relocation mode until one additional instruction is executed. This gives the control program the opportunity to transfer control to the operational program. Otherwise, the transfer of control instruction would itself be incremented. When relocation mode is used in conjunction with memory protection mode, comparison with the boundary registers occurs after addresses have been incremented by the relocation register.

PROGRAM FRAGMENTATION

The organization of memory in the form of a list structure causes programs to be broken up into blocks located in different parts of memory. This fragmentation would tend to occur even if the list technique were not used, due to the irregular sizes of programs and the differing amounts of time they remain in core. Furthermore, each program's entry block and associated data areas are scattered through memory.

The methods for memory protection and program relocation just described are effective only where all parts of a program, i.e., instructions, constants, work areas, and data, are contiguous. Otherwise, continual references outside of the protected area would occur, resulting in frequent traps. Furthermore, incrementation by the relocation register would not result in the addressing of the proper locations.

A technique for memory protection and program relocation for fragmented operational programs could be provided by using multiple boundary registers, each pair of which would be associated with a relocation register. As a simple illustration consider a program fragmented into two parts. Assume that all data, constants, and working areas are contained in these two areas of core storage. The machine has boundary registers 1, relocation register 1, boundary registers 2, and relocation register 2. Let the program consist of 9775 words placed in memory as follows:

1st fragment in 2123–6457	4335 words
2nd fragment in 13471–18910	5440 words
	9775 words

The following illustration shows the program before and after being brought into core, and how it is executed.

	Compiled as			Placed in core			Executed as		
	00000	CLA	00100	02123	CLA	00100	02123	CLA	02223
	00001	TRA	00150	02124	TRA	00150	02124	TRA	00150
	.	.	.	.	.	.	.	.	.
	.	.	.	.	.	.	.	.	.
	.	.	.	.	.	.	.	.	.
	00150	STO	00125	02273	STO	00125	02273	STO	02248
	00151	CLA	05872	02274	CLA	05872	02274	CLA	15007
	.	.	.	.	.	.	.	.	.
	.	.	.	.	.	.	.	.	.
	.	.	.	.	.	.	.	.	.
Start of 2nd segment	04335	CLA	08000	13471	CLA	08000	13471	CLA	17135
	04336	TRA	00151	13472	TRA	00151	13472	TRA	00151†
	.	.	.	.	.	.	.	.	.
	.	.	.	.	.	.	.	.	.
	.	.	.	.	.	.	.	.	.

† Effectively causes a transfer to location 02274.

Before control is transferred to this program, boundary registers 1 are loaded with an upper bound of 4334 and a lower bound of 0000.

In relocation register 1 is placed 2123. The control program loads boundary registers 2 with an upper bound of 9775 and a lower bound of 4335. Relocation register 2 receives 9136 (13471 − 4335). The control program transfers control to location 0000. The program is compiled with its origin at 0000.

Here is how the procedure works: An operand is first compared with boundary registers 1. If the address lies within these limits, it is incremented by relocation register 1. Transfer-type orders are not incremented. However, the instruction counter is first compared with boundary registers 1. If the address is within these limits, it is incremented by relocation register 1.

When an address lies outside of boundary registers 1, it is automatically compared with boundary registers 2. If within the limits of boundary registers 2, the address is incremented by relocation register 2. If an address is outside of the bounds of both boundary registers 1 and 2, an interrupt back to the control program occurs.

This technique permits transfers of control back and forth between program segments. For example, when the instruction counter is stepped to 4335, it is now outside of the first segment of the program, and is, therefore, outside of boundary registers 1. IC is now compared with boundary registers 2. It is within these limits, and is hence incremented by relocation register 2, which contains 9136. The effective address of IC thus becomes 13471, the first instruction in the second segment of the program.

Similarly, when IC reaches 04336, the instruction in 13472 is fetched. This is a transfer to 00151. The address 00151 is not incremented, so the instruction is executed as TRA 00151. Now, however, IC is reset to 00151. This causes the machine to fetch the instruction located at 02274, which is back in the first segment.

One difficulty with this technique is that the comparison with the boundary registers might slow up the computer. This problem could be circumvented by having the equipment perform these comparisons in parallel.

The question arises as to how many sets of boundary and relocation registers are needed. It is obvious that these registers are used only for the operational program currently being executed. When the control program decides to give control to another program, the control program refills these registers with different constants. Therefore, the number of sets of boundary and relocation registers required is equal to the number needed by the most fragmented program.

THE ONE-LEVEL STORE

The one-level store technique developed for the Atlas computer at the University of Manchester in England solves the problems of memory protection and program relocation with fragmented programs. Here is an illustration of how it might work:

Let us consider all of core and disk storage to be composed of blocks or "pages" of 256 words. There are 2^{18} blocks in the entire system. If we assume that there are available 2^7 blocks of core storage, only 2^7 of the 2^{18} pages can be in core at any given time. Each page has a number, and a directory of the pages is maintained in core storage. The programmer addresses only the directory. He does not know whether the page he addresses is in core or not at the time an instruction is about to be executed. Whenever a page is in core, its number is entered into a word in the directory, along with the absolute location of the block in core it is occupying. The directory consists of 128 words—one word for each available core block. The format of the words in the directory is:

Number of page (18 bits)	Location of page in core storage (7 bits)	Status bits

An address in an instruction consists of 26 bits, of which the first 18 constitute the page number, and the last eight the specific word in the addressed page.

To execute an instruction, the machine must first find the requested page. This is done by searching the directory, using the 18-bit page number in the address of the instruction as the argument. If the requested page is in core, its page number will be in the directory, and the proper word in that block is obtained by using the eight-bit word number in the address part of the instruction. If the page is not in memory, an interrupt to the control program occurs. The control program computes the disk address of the page, and proceeds to read this requested block into core. An entry is now made in the directory so that later requests for this page will find that it is in core.

Searching the directory by conventional means would be highly time consuming. For this reason, the directory would probably consist of an associative memory. This type of memory is content-addressed —the equipment locates the word corresponding to the page number immediately. Hence, no search is necessary.

There is no problem of program relocation in a one-level store. All instructions calling for input-output operations and halts cause an interrupt to the control program, as do illegal operation codes. When shift-type instructions occur, the directory is not involved. Before an instruction is fetched, the number in IC is looked up in the directory. If the page containing an instruction is not in core, the control program initiates an input operation.

Memory protection is achieved by program-identification bits in the instruction word. These must match program-identification bits associated with page numbers in the directory.

Several status bits are necessary for the operation of a one-level store. A lock-out bit designates that the control program has initiated reading in a requested block, but that this page cannot yet be referenced, as the input operation is still under way.

Another status bit prevents writing out a page which has not been modified by a program. This is necessary because there are sometimes no unused block areas in core which can be allocated to pages read in from disks. Hence, the control program must select some page to write out to make room for the requested page. However, if the selected page has not been altered since it was read in, this same page still exists on the disk. Therefore, the core copy need not be saved; it is simply read over when the requested page is read into core. The decision as to which page to write out when core space is needed is made by a replacement algorithm.

5 THE LIFE OF A TRANSACTION IN SABRE

Whenever an agent enters information into the Sabre system, he actuates the terminal set to enter a transaction code into the message. This code tells the control program to call upon the particular operational program needed to process this input. Often an entry requires the services of a complex of operational programs. Each segment of an operational program requests its successor. Similarly, each operational program calls upon or gives control to other programs. It is possible for an operational program to make an entry in the CPU queue.

The nature of an airline reservation system requires operational programs to make frequent disk and drum requests. Access to these files is slow, and programs are often unable to proceed until the requested I/O operation is complete. When a program is stalled, it gives control back to the control program, which then allocates the CPU to another program.

Whenever a program surrenders control, or is interrupted, the address in the instruction counter and the contents of various registers and indicators are stored. Otherwise, the information is destroyed. Data are restored to a program when it resumes execution. The storage of IC permits the control program to know the instruction to which control must be transferred when the program regains use of the CPU. In actuality, what is saved is not the instruction counter, but rather the relative location of the instruction in the program segment. The relative location is used because the program segment may have to be read

47

into core again, and it may be allocated a different block in storage on this second occasion. Therefore, although the program may resume execution from a different absolute location, the relative location in the program segment is the same.

In the 7090, the saving of IC and other information must be programmed. However, it may be worthwhile in other machines to build in an instruction which stores all of the registers and indicators at once, rather than to use several instructions for this purpose. In the case of an I/O interrupt in the 7090, the contents of the instruction counter are placed automatically in a special core location. This address is then moved by program to a permanent memory cell; otherwise, it is destroyed by the next interrupt.

As we have seen, an entry block is a region in core which holds an original message and all later information used and generated by its operational programs during the "life" of the transaction. One function of the entry block is to hold information during the time between its surrender of control and its resumption of execution. This period is called a *wait*. In the Mercury system, a specified storage area for such information is associated with each program waiting to resume. However, in Sabre a storage area must be associated with each entry. The reason for this difference is that in Mercury only one input at a time can use an operational program, whereas in Sabre two or more transactions can employ the same program simultaneously. For example, assume that a given program is stalled awaiting a disk access, while processing entry X. Before the disk operation is complete, entry Y requests the same program. The control program gives control to Y, which may conceivably get ahead of X in the program. Indeed, Y could well finish using the program before the processing of X was resumed. Therefore, each entry must have its own storage area.

In Sabre, no dynamic program modification is permitted over waits. That is to say, programmers are forbidden to modify a program during its execution if it is possible for that program to lose control of the CPU through requesting an I/O operation. The reason for this restriction is that if a program changed its own instructions, after which it yielded control, another entry might use the same program. However, the second entry would now be processed by improper instructions. Even if the program initialized itself, trouble could arise if the second entry got ahead of the first entry in utilizing the program. In this event, the first entry, when it was resumed, could be using erroneous instructions.

Where a program never undergoes a wait, there is no possibility of a second entry using the same program. Here dynamic program modification is permissible. By the way, when a program loses control because of a trap, this is not equivalent to a wait. When the interrupt subroutine ends, it returns control to the program, and there is no opportunity for another entry to make use of the program during the intervening period.

STORING INFORMATION IN AN ENTRY BLOCK

Whenever a program contains a possible branch where control might be surrendered, any information which might ordinarily be reflected in program modification must be stored in the entry block. To store data in an entry block, operational programs use the RENTS macro. This subroutine makes available in an entry block the space requested by the program. The number of words needed is specified by the program when it employs the RENTS macro.

Situations frequently arise where a number of areas must be *rented* in an entry block. This occurs when there are numerous levels of nesting of operational programs. For example, program A transfers to program B, which transfers to C. When program C terminates, it transfers back to B. In turn, when B ends, it gives control to program A. Ten levels of nesting are permitted in Sabre. The return location for each program in the nest is stored in the entry block. In a nest, several programs may rent words. The entry block keeps their information during the periods when they lose control.

Rented space may also be used to communicate among the various programs used to process an entry. Where a chain of programs processes an input, two or more of the programs may need to share intermediate data in common. This is achieved by giving each program using the data the address of the rented space. To enable all of the programs to locate the common area, this address is passed on from one program to another.

Many areas in an entry block may be rented at the same time. Each time an area is rented, the control program acquires, for its own purpose, one word following that area. In this control word it places the number of words which have just been rented. When a program no longer needs an area it has rented, it employs the FENTS macro to release the rented area, i.e., to make it available for use again. The control word enables the control program to release the proper number of rented words. The FENTS macro releases only the area last rented. Hence, rented areas are deleted progressively, one by one, until the first program to obtain an area releases this area with FENTS.

When an entry is completely processed, the program must call upon the EXIT macro. This subroutine "blasts" the entry block and everything associated with it. Since there is no further need for all of the information associated with the transaction, it is destroyed. As we have seen, deletion simply means that the blocks allocated to the entry are returned to the available block list. All rented areas are, of course, blasted when the entry block is deleted.

In some instances a transaction requires more rented space than is available in the entry block. If this occurs, the RENTS subroutine obtains another block of core from the available block list, and chains this block to the entry block. This additional block is used for renting the required space.

Where an additional block is withdrawn from the available block list by RENTS, it is good practice for the programmer to release his rented space with FENTS, rather than waiting for EXIT to perform this task. The reason is that since core space is limited, the sooner it returns to the available block list, the more memory is usable for other purposes. FENTS releases a rented area immediately. If FENTS is not used, rented area may remain unavailable unnecessarily until the entry terminates (which may not occur for a relatively long time).

Rather than renting space, a programmer may obtain additional core by using macros such as GET. These subroutines obtain available blocks, and chain them directly to the entry block. One occasion when an entire block is needed is when a program requests a table of data or some record from the drums or disks. Before these I/O requests are initiated, a subroutine in the control program obtains a block of core into which the data can be placed when it arrives. This block is chained to the transaction's entry block.

Chaining to entry blocks makes use of push-down lists with back references. Each block added to the chain is placed at the top of the list, and contains a pointer to the previous block appended to the chain. The entry block maintains a base word which holds the address of the last block appended and the number of blocks in the entire list. Programs can delete blocks by employing macros. All chained blocks are released by EXIT.

When needed, entry blocks are obtained from the available block list, and are returned to this list after the transaction is complete. One of the words in the entry block serves as a pointer when it is on the available block list. As we shall see, this pointer word is also used to chain the entry block to the real-time ready and working lists, as well as the CPU ready and working lists.

THE LIFE OF TRANSACTIONS

While an operational program is processing a transaction, it must have some way of communicating with that transaction's entry block. Therefore, whenever the control program gives control to an operational program, the control program places the address of its transaction's entry block in a fixed core location called ENWO (entry word). The program can now use this address to reference the entry block. For convenience, the address of the last rented area in this entry block is also placed in another fixed location (ENWO + 1). Now the program in control can obtain the address of this rented region easily.

In discussing the CPU list program, we spoke of adding or deleting programs from the real-time ready, real-time working, CPU ready, and CPU working queues. Actually what is done is to add or delete entry blocks from these queues. When a message enters the system, it is placed in an entry block, and this entry block goes on the real-time ready queue, from which list it later moves to the real-time working queue. When a program is stalled, this fact is recorded in the entry block of the transaction being processed. When the I/O operation ends, an indication that the entry block is ready to resume is placed on the CPU ready list, and is later moved to the CPU working list.

In actuality, of course, entry blocks are never physically moved about in memory. They are located at random in various areas of core. Queues of entry blocks are created by using the list technique. The pointer word in the entry block is employed for this purpose.

What essentially happens when the CPU is reassigned by the control program is a transfer of control from one transaction's current program to some other transaction's current program. The CPU life of an entry consists of an intermittent series of opportunities for that transaction's program complex to make use of the central processing unit. When an entry's program does not have control of the CPU, that program is either waiting for an I/O operation to be initiated or completed, or is standing by, completely idle, on a CPU list, waiting to be resumed.

THE FIND AND WAIT MACROS

An operational program requests I/O operations by macros such as FIND, which obtains a record from a disk. These subroutines enter requests on the appropriate I/O queues, and then return control to the requesting program. The program need not relinquish control at this time. It may well be that the program is able to continue executing more instructions before it will need the requested data from the disk. That is why the I/O subroutine returns control to the requesting program. When a program cannot proceed further without requested I/O data, it employs the WAIT macro. WAIT yields control of the CPU. When I/O is complete, the control program places this program's entry block on the CPU ready list.

If there is a long intervening sequence of instructions between FIND and WAIT, the input-output requested by FIND may already have been completed by the time WAIT is called upon. If this is the case, WAIT causes a transfer of control back to the program which gave the WAIT. It may be more advantageous for a programmer to give a WAIT many instructions after his FIND. Indeed, he might wish to give a WAIT several program segments after the segment in which he employed FIND. This would enable his programs to execute more instructions in the intervening period.

A bit position is reserved in the entry block to record a WAIT. If the requested input-output is incomplete when this bit is set, the program loses control, and the control program places the transaction on the CPU ready list when the FIND is finished. On the other hand, if the WAIT bit is turned on after the I/O is complete, then, as we have stated, the program which just gave the WAIT receives control immediately without being placed on the CPU ready list.

A program does not know whether or not its requested data have arrived satisfactorily in core until it calls upon WAIT. Hence, it would be impossible for a program to make use of this data without giving a WAIT.

In some instances, an operational program may require more than one item of information from the disks or drums before it can proceed with an entry. In such cases, the programmer issues as many FINDS as necessary, followed by a WAIT. The control program cannot place this transaction on the CPU ready list until it services all of the I/O requests. For if the transaction's program were given control again, with one or more requests uninitiated or incomplete, the program would not be able to resume properly. A mechanism in the control program prevents this from occurring. Every time a FIND is used, an I/O counter in the entry block is incremented by one. Whenever a request is completed, this counter is decreased by one. Only when the state of the counter is zero does the control program place the entry block on the CPU ready list. By the way, the subroutine which reduces the I/O counter operates with interrupts disabled. If trapping were not prevented, a second interrupt from a completed I/O operation could interfere with the execution of the subroutine.

FILE REQUESTS

When FIND is executed, it places the file request in a seven-word block on the queue for the disk or drum which contains the information. A separate queue is maintained for each I/O unit to assist the control program in immediately initiating another request for a unit as soon as the previous request is complete. When an input request terminates, the trap transfers control to an interrupt subroutine in the control program. This subroutine initiates a SEEK for the next item (if any) on that I/O unit's queue. At this time, it also takes the opportunity to initiate SEEKS for items on the other I/O unit queues which have been waiting for the channel to be free.

The seven-word block used for I/O queues is drawn from the pool of available blocks. FIND places in these seven words all of the information necessary to obtain the proper record from the files and to make this record available at some later time to the transaction's program. One of the words contains the input command which is sent to the channel. The address part of another of the words is used to point to the next seven-word block in the queue.

After a file request is complete, the control program places the requesting transaction's entry block on the CPU ready list (assuming that entry has no other requests outstanding). It is not possible to predict when a request will be fulfilled. The question arises: When an input is completed, how does the control program know which entry block is connected with that input? This problem is solved as follows: When FIND is called upon, it obtains from ENWO the address of the entry block associated with the requesting program. This address is placed in the seven-word block. When the input is later complete, the control program can get the address of the input's associated entry block from its seven-word block. But how is the completed input associated with its seven-word block? The interrupt program identifies channels because they trap to different core locations. The I/O unit which caused the trap is identified by an instruction which stores in core the location + 1 of the command given originally to the channel. This information enables the trap subroutine to locate the seven-word block which originated the file request. Now the interrupt subroutine can ascertain which entry block is associated with the input. The subroutine next reduces the I/O counter in this entry block, and proceeds as described previously.

When an entry regains control after having a file request completed, how does its program know where in core this information has been placed by FIND? Here is the answer: When the operational program gives a FIND, the program must specify a rented word into which the address of the arriving record is placed by the control program. The core address of the record requested by FIND is thus placed in rented storage. When the program resumes processing after its file request has been completed, it can thus obtain the address of the block into which the desired record was read.

ALLOCATION OF STORAGE TO INPUTS

We must now consider how the control program reserves a block for a requested file record. Since core space is in short supply, it would be poor practice for FIND to reserve a block each time it places a request on an input queue. It may take a relatively long time for a request to rise to the top of a queue and to be initiated. During this period, the reserved block would serve no purpose, and would be unavailable for other needs. Therefore, the task of reserving blocks for I/O requests is given to the I/O interrupt subroutines. Whenever a trap occurs at the completion of an input request, the interrupt subroutine obtains a block of storage from the available pool, and assigns this block to the next file request in the queue. This is done by placing the address of the assigned block in the request's seven-word block on the queue. After the block is allocated, the interrupt program initiates the request. In this way, blocks are withdrawn from the available list only when immediately necessary.

The channel command specifies into which block of core the channel is to place the input record. After its arrival, the interrupt subroutine chains the record's block to the requesting transaction's entry block. The record is available to the transaction's programs during the life of the entry, or until released by one of the operational programs processing the transaction. The control program returns these blocks to the available list when an EXIT is given. In the case of output requests for disks or drums, the operational program gives the macro FILE the core address of the block to be written, along with its destination. When transmission has been satisfactorily completed, a trap occurs, and the next output request is initiated by an interrupt subroutine. Since the block containing the record just written is needed no longer, this interrupt subroutine releases it to the available list.

ASSEMBLY OF DATA FROM TERMINALS

After an agent sells a seat on a flight, he obtains the passenger's name, telephone number, address, and numerous other items of information. All of this data enters the machine system, which places it in a passenger name record in the files for future reference.

Since the agent receives his data gradually, in the course of a telephone conversation with the passenger, the agent has to enter this passenger information into the terminal in piecemeal fashion. For this reason, an agent's assembly area (AAA) is used to assemble each passenger name record. The AAA is a blank block with a fixed format for passenger data. The machine prepares the passenger name record by editing and shifting about the information in the AAA.

Although an agent can enter data for only one customer at a time, many agents may be actively communicating with the computer simultaneously. Therefore, one AAA must be available for every terminal in the system. The Sabre system makes use of about 1100 agents' assembly areas. Since all of the AAA's obviously cannot be kept permanently in core, they are stored on the drums, which provide a faster access than the disks. Certain permanent information pertaining to its terminal remains permanently in each AAA.

The drum location of each AAA is an absolute address which is computable from the address of the terminal. When an agent begins to enter passenger data, the drum address of his AAA is calculated, and a drum request is initiated. The address which the AAA will occupy in core is placed in the entry block. To avoid repeated computation of the drum address, it is also stored in the entry block for use while additional information comes in from the agent. Each entry transmitted to core from the terminal contains a code identifying where it belongs in the AAA. Studies of the conversation between the agent and the customer show that many seconds elapse between each item elicited from the customer by the agent. Because of the limited amount of core storage available, this is too long a period for the AAA to be kept in main memory. Therefore, after each field is inserted into the AAA, the AAA is written back on the drum. Whenever the agent enters another item, the AAA is obtained again from the drum.

In some instances, so much passenger information must be entered by an agent into the system that there is an overflow from the AAA. In such cases, an additional block can be chained to the AAA.

It is possible for an agent to change an entry in the AAA while the passenger information is being assembled. He can enter items into the AAA in random order. When he has finished transmitting data into the machine system, the agent presses an *end transaction* key. This causes the computer to check the AAA for missing information. If any items are lacking, the machine sends a message to the agent, requesting this data. As has been stated, after all of the information has been assembled, the computer packs the items in the AAA into a passenger name record which is then stored on the disks.

Akin to the AAA is the deferred cancellation area (DXA). When a customer calls up to cancel a reservation, the agent enters the cancellation data in this area. After the agent has finished transmitting this information, he presses the end transaction button, at which time the computer cancels the reservation. The DXA is used because customers frequently change their minds about canceling. If the AAA were used for canceling, the canceled seat would be returned immediately to inventory prior to the completion of this transaction. If the flight were then sold out, the customer would not be able to regain his seat if he changed his mind about canceling. By employing the DXA, the seat is not returned immediately to inventory, and hence is still available if the passenger decides not to cancel after all.

TRANSFER OF CONTROL TO ANOTHER SEGMENT

What happens when one segment of an operational program transfers control to another segment? Certain operational programs are kept permanently in core, whereas others are stored on the drum. Hence, when a segment transfers control, the next segment may be in core or may be on the drums.

A routine in the control program handles transfers to segments stored on the drum. This procedure maintains a list of core storage available for retrieved segments. Since a transfer to a next segment may call upon a segment which was read previously from drums to core because it was needed by another entry, the control program must keep track of which requested segments are already in core and which must be retrieved from the drums. Where there is more than one demand for a next segment, a queue must be maintained for all of these requests. The control program must ascertain whether core storage is available for a demanded segment, and must keep a list of entries waiting for core storage for their requested program segment. When a block of core becomes available, it is assigned to demanded segments. When a segment is no longer needed, its core space is returned to the available list. Since segments temporarily not in demand (because they have transferred control to a next segment) occupy needed blocks of storage, their space is made available for segments which are currently in demand.

Three macros are used to transfer control from one segment to a next segment:

(1) ENTERN   Transfer to next segment with no return to previous segment.

(2) ENTER   Transfer to next segment with return to previous segment.

(3) BACK   Return to previous segment.

At the time when programmers are assigned to write operational programs, it has probably not yet been decided which operational programs will be kept permanently in core and which will be maintained on the drums. This decision can only be made after it is known how much core will be available for storage of operational programs. The amount of such available storage is a function of numerous variables, such as the number of entry blocks and chained data blocks which will be in use, the size of the control program, and the frequency with which segments kept on the drums will be needed. These factors are in turn dependent upon the input loads which will be placed upon the system at various times. Therefore, the decision as to where to store operational programs must be delayed until more is known about how core storage will be utilized during actual operation.

Hence, programmers are not able at the time of writing their programs to specify where the next segment is located when they transfer control from one segment to another. A post-processor is therefore used after program compilation to convert the above macros to macros which specify the whereabouts of demanded segments.

The macro ENTER is converted to:

(a) ENTRA   A segment from core or from drum transfers to a segment on drum, with return to itself.

(b) ENTRB   A segment from drum transfers to a core segment, with return to itself.

The macro ENTERN is converted to:

(a) ENTN   A segment from core or from drum transfers to a segment on drum, with no return to itself.

(b) ENTCN   A segment from drum transfers to a core segment, with no return to itself.

The post-processor places absolute core locations in the macro if a transfer to a core program occurs. Segment number and entry point in segment are given where a transfer to a segment kept on the drums is requested.

When these macros are executed, a number of logical possibilities arise. For example, ENTRA places in the entry block the address in the present segment to which the next segment must later transfer control back. Now there are three alternatives:

(1) Control must be transferred to a drum segment which is presently in core.

(2) Control must be transferred to a drum segment which is not in core.

(3) Control must be transferred to a drum segment which has already been demanded by a segment of another operational program.

As has been stated, core areas used for segments must be returned to the available storage list as soon as possible after the segment has been used. There are two levels of immediacy of return to the available storage list. The *high-priority* level contains those blocks which are the first to be used when storage for segments is needed. After all of the high-priority blocks have been allocated, *low-priority* blocks are used. The distinction between levels is based on the following condition: When a macro specifies no return to the previous segment, that segment's block is placed in the high-priority group, unless that segment is in demand by another segment. If in demand, the block gets low priority, since it may shortly be used. Macros specifying return to a previous segment are treated in a similar way.

The system for handling all of the logical possibilities for all of the macros is based on several tables which contain such information as the core location of segments read in from the drums; a tally of the number of segments demanding a particular segment; an indication of whether a segment's core area is available; queues of requests for segment storage area; and lists of requests which have been assigned core storage, but which are waiting for retrieval from a drum.

STORAGE ALLOCATION WITH 7080's

Since IBM 7080's have no index registers, it is not feasible to relocate programs. Therefore, all programs are executed from a fixed place in core storage. A special area in memory is allocated for the storage of any program about to be processed. All programs are assembled so as to run from these locations. This program processing area consists of 1200 character positions. In the 7080, there are 5 characters per instruction. Actually only 237 instructions can be placed in this region.

When a program is needed, the control program moves the program into the program processing area. A number of contiguous regions in memory are reserved for associated information. These locations include:

(a) A region where the entry block is kept while the entry's program is executed.

(b) Six request word areas. These are memory locations used to receive information requested from the files. The contents of the request word areas are lost over a departure (WAIT) macro, unless the program specifies that they be saved.

(c) A temporary storage area. This region is not preserved over a departure macro.

(d) Two other areas which contain data associated permanently with the entry during its life in the machine.

When an entry yields control, the areas to be saved, including the entry block itself, are moved elsewhere in memory. When the entry regains control, the control program moves these blocks back into the program execution area. The operational programmer need not be concerned with the mechanics of moving his program and its associated information in and out of the program execution area. He can always assume that his entry block, working storage, and other information are in the proper locations for execution. The analysis block, used for testing purposes under the option of the programmer (see page 157), is moved back and forth from the program execution area along with the other information. A special memory protection device prevents a running program from addressing any part of memory outside of the program execution area.

7080 ENTRY BLOCKS

Each entry block has an input message area. This region, consisting of 110 characters, retains the message during the entire life of the entry.

The entry block also contains a request word control area. When a program wants the control program to save the information in one or more of the six request word areas, it informs the control program of this requirement by means of indicators set in the request word control area. Block control areas control levels of nesting of operational programs.

Each entry block has a 150-character operational storage area which is retained throughout the life of the entry. Hence, it can be used for intercommunication among the operational programs processing a particular entry. The first 135 character positions in the operational storage area are unassigned. The other 15 positions are restricted to various purposes. For example, characters 136-144 are used for setting program switches. Since four bits in each position are usable for this purpose, these nine positions provide 36 switches. Position 145 of the operational storage area is used as an error indicator switch. The six bits comprising this character are initialized at the outset. These bits serve as indicators of an error return from an operational program. Here is an illustration of such an error: Assume program A enters program B. Program A was required to supply certain information to B. Suppose that B is not able to find the proper data, and is unable to continue. All that program B can do at this point is to return to A, setting an error indicator as it does so. When program A receives control it tests the error indicator, and decides what to do.

SIMULTANEOUS UPDATING OF THE SAME RECORD

During the same period of time, it is possible for two entries to request the identical record from the disks or drums. If one or both of the transactions alter the record, a logical error might result. For example, suppose entry A obtains and updates a disk record. Assume that entry B now requests the same record before transaction A returns its record to the files. In this event, B uses the same record as A. Hence, B operates on incorrect information and may write erroneous data back on the disk. To avoid such situations, a programmer can *hold* a record obtained from the files. This prevents other programs from requesting this record until it is *unheld* by the original requesting program. The control program keeps a list of all held items by placing indicators in the disk and drum request queues.

At American Airlines, a program exercises a hold by including a tag in the FIND macro. This causes the control program to search the appropriate input request queue for the presence of a previous hold on the record. If the item is not being held, the request is initiated, and the record now enters hold status. Where a program is already holding an item, other programs requesting the record remain stalled until the hold is removed.†

If a FIND does not include a hold tag, the control program permits other programs to read a held record. The assumption here is that the programmer who used the FIND must have decided that no harm could result by giving these other programs access to the item.

† Under certain circumstances, circular holds may develop. This logical problem is discussed on page 159.

In a system where multiple computers shared the processing load one of the problems would be that two or more machines could request the identical record during the same period of time. To avoid this possibility, some intercomputer communication procedure would have to be established to enable each machine to ascertain whether a requested record was already in hold status. It would probably be impractical for each computer to interrogate the others every time it wished to initiate a disk request. Another technique might be to maintain a common list of held records, but this procedure could also be time consuming.

MACHINE ERRORS AND PROGRAM ERRORS

Since there is no memory protection in Sabre, it would be possible for an undebugged program error to cause difficulties. In a minor instance, such an error would merely cause the execution of an improper procedure. But a serious error could cause a program to run wild, altering other transactions' data, distorting other programs, transferring into peculiar locations, or causing data words to operate as instructions. Machine errors could produce similar effects.

In the worst possible case, that in which core memory would be wiped out or rendered completely useless, the Sabre system would not be seriously disturbed. What would happen is simply that each entry the machine was working on would be destroyed. In this event, each agent who initiated a transaction would fail to receive a response from the computer. If this should occur, such agents, acting in accordance with standard operating procedures, would resubmit their entries into the system. By this time, the control program will have been reloaded, and the computer would process the re-entered inputs in the usual way.

It is true that inaccuracies could result if, in the course of processing an entry, an operational program updated an inventory record, and if core memory was destroyed before a confirmation was sent back to the agent. It is believed that such occurrences would merely cause slight imbalances in the seat inventory which would be of very minor importance in the operation of the airline. To correct such errors, a daily reconciliation program will be run, which will check the number of passenger name records for each flight against the total reservations for each flight.

In the event of machine failure or serious program error, a halt will ultimately occur. If the internal alarm clock is not reset every 500 milliseconds, a whistle alerts the operator to take action. Hence, the presence of such errors is recognized within half a second. If the machine is malfunctioning, switchover to the other computer is manually initiated. When the backup machine is interrupted while executing a nonreal-time program, conventional breakpoint procedures for the batch program will be followed.

One 7080 real-time system has an automatic switchover procedure. Here, both 7080's are connected together via channels. At regular intervals a clock interrupts both machines simultaneously. At this time, the off-line machine sends an interrogation to the other processor. If the off-line computer does not receive an answer, it assumes that the on-line machine is not running, and the off-line computer takes over the real-time operation.

Automatic switchover is much more rapid than a manual method, which requires deliberation, diagnosis, and actions by an operator. In the above system, for example, if an error is occurring in input transmission, either the 7080 is at fault, or a 7750. It is easier for the switchover program to trace which unit is in error and to make the appropriate switchover than for a human to carry out these procedures.

At the Mercury computational center, both machines have their own DCC 7281, channels, tapes, and other peripheral equipment. The computers are kept running in parallel, processing the same data. However, only one of the machines transmits outputs to the Cape Kennedy Mercury Control Center. There is no communication between the computers. Switchover from one machine to another simply consists of disconnecting one machine from the transmission lines to Cape Kennedy, and connecting the other. This is done by means of switching relays.

The decision to switch from one machine to another is made by the flight controllers, and is based on the examination of printouts and displays. If the computer supplying outputs generates calculations which deviate unusually from expected values, it is assumed that this machine is malfunctioning, and the decision is made to switch over. By the way, both computers do not run completely simultaneously, for the outputting machine tends to fall behind the other computer by a matter of milliseconds, as a result of the time it takes to transmit messages to Cape Kennedy.

The restart procedure in Mercury consists of writing out each spacecraft position vector on a tape each time this calculation is made.

To restart a computer, core is reloaded, and the vectors are brought in from the tape. These past calculations enable the machine to build up a new orbit table very rapidly, i.e., to develop another set of predictions of the spacecraft's position.

No attempt is made to protect core memory from being incorrectly addressed and changed by an erroneous program. The assumption is that all programs have been completely debugged, and that memory protection is therefore unnecessary. An improper memory reference caused by a machine error results in deviations detectable in the print-outs and displays.

In planning the Mercury computing system, it was noted that additional reliability can be attained by minimizing the use of tapes. For this reason, tape operations were reduced to four main operations:

(1) Initial loading of core.
(2) Reading in the next set of programs at the end of a phase.
(3) Logging the entire flight.
(4) Restarting the system in the event of temporary machine errors.

Each machine has three channels, among which tape operations are spread in order to increase the overlapping of input-output. Backup tape units on each channel can be used if one of the other channels becomes inoperative.

6 PRIORITY PROCESSING IN PROJECT MERCURY

PRIORITIES AMONG PROGRAMS

About 40 programs are directly employed in the real-time system used for the Mercury project. These include input-edit routines, tele-type code conversion routines, coordinate conversion routines, output generators, a retrofire calculation routine, a differential correction program, and a numerical integration program. The usual sequence of data processing is input validation, editing, orbit correction, orbit integrations, and output computations. If the editing program finds excessively deviant radar data, it alters this normal sequence. There are more than 20 different inputs, each with its own interrupt sub-routine.

There are two major ways in which Mercury differs from a real-time commercial data processing system:

(1) All of the programs urgently needed during a particular phase of the project can be kept simultaneously in core memory. After each phase of the Mercury operation, a new set of programs is read into core. Hence, there is no need to read additional program segments into memory continually, as in the airline reservation systems.

(2) No large files of information are required. Disks and drums, therefore, are not needed, and there is no corresponding problem of idle CPU time while I/O requests are under way.†

---

† This is not true in the Mercury Gemini system. In the Mercury system, it was later found that all of the operational programs could not be kept in core simultaneously, as originally planned. Of course, in some commercial real-time systems, all of the programs can be kept in core at the same time.

However, Mercury has one feature not usually present in most business applications. An elaborate, continually changing set of priorities must be assigned to the programs. Since certain inputs must be processed immediately, the programs associated with such inputs are executed, even if another program has not terminated. Simple examples of this requirement are interrupt subroutines. These must be executed prior to the interrupted program to prevent the loss of real-time input information.

Priority requirements among programs which process or handle data generate interleaving of programs or partially completed programs. Display programs, for instance, have a higher priority than many other operational programs. These programs are initiated at appropriate times by a real-time clock included in the equipment. This clock interrupts whatever program is running, transferring control to a monitor (control program). Now a decision is made whether to execute the display program, or to continue with the interrupted program. The control program decides how to proceed by consulting a table containing the priority relations among the operational programs.

Sometimes it is necessary for one operational program to prevent another program of higher priority from obtaining control. For example, suppose program X gets control and commences a tape operation. During this operation, it is possible for program X to be interrupted, and for control to be given to program Y. However, if Y makes use of the same tape as X, this transfer of control to Y could interfere with X's tape operation. Therefore, as soon as X gets control, one of its first actions is to suppress Y. The ability of one operational program to suppress another makes it possible for preassigned priorities to be changed, in effect, while the system is running.

THE PRIORITY MECHANISM

The priority table consists of a list of operational programs, arranged in order of priority. Three indicators, denoted by A, B, and C, are associated with each program in the table. A program turns its A indicator on when it first gets control, and turns its A indicator off when it is finished. A B indicator is turned on whenever an input requiring a program is entered into that program's queue of waiting results. When a program's input queue is emptied, the program turns off its B indicator. A program's C indicator is turned on when that program is suppressed by another program. The function of these indicators will become clearer as we proceed. In general, A means *in process, B* means *ready to be started,* and *C* means *suppress.* Since a program can be suppressed for various reasons, indicator *C* actually consists of more than one field.

Operational programs always run in the *enabled* mode, and in this respect have a lower priority than the interrupt routines. After a trap occurs, the control program searches the priority table for the highest priority unsuppressed program which is either waiting to be resumed after an interruption, or which has inputs waiting to be processed. As has been stated, an operational program's position in the table determines its priority. The control program seeks the first operational program in the table with an *A* or *B* indicator on, or both. This program obtains control, unless its *C* indicator is on. If *C* is on, this operational program is suppressed, and the control program continues to scan the priority table.

If the highest priority unsuppressed operational program has only its *A* indicator on, this means that this program once had control, but was not executed completely because of an interrupt. Therefore, the control program returns control to the next instruction after the instruction where the trap occurred. The address of this instruction was saved when the control counter was stored at the time of the interrupt. When a program terminates, it turns off its *A* indicator, and transfers back to the control program.

If the highest priority unsuppressed operational program has only its *B* indicator on, this signifies that one or more inputs are waiting to be processed by this program. The control program gives control in this case to the first instruction in the operational program. Whenever a program removes the last item from its input queue, the program turns off its *B* indicator.

If the first highest priority unsuppressed operational program has both its *A* and *B* indicators on, this means that this program was interrupted when it still had at least one item left in its input queue.

The lowest priority program in the system is DIAG, a diagnostic program which is executed whenever the CPU has nothing else to do. Typically, DIAG runs until the filling of an input buffer by the real-time channel causes a trap. The interrupt routine now moves the input out of the buffer area, places it in the queue for the required program, turns on this program's *B* indicator, and gives control to the control program. The control program searches the priority table, finds that this program is the highest priority unsuppressed program, and accordingly transfers control to its first instruction.

THE OPERATION OF THE PRIORITY MECHANISM

This situation is shown in the following diagram.† Here is depicted a sequence of nineteen events and their effect on the computing system. In this simplified situation, it is assumed that there are four operational programs, Z, Y, X, and W, plus DIAG, in the system. Program Z has the highest preassigned priority, and is followed by Y, X, and W. Program W has the lowest priority, except for DIAG. The list of inputs waiting to be processed by Y appears in the right-hand column.

The system starts at event 1. Since there have been no real-time inputs thus far, there is no input queue on any of the programs; hence, no B indicators are on. Event 2 is an interrupt requiring program X. Accordingly, X's B indicator is turned on. In event 3, the control program gives control to X. X immediately turns on its A indicator. As the queue for X is empty now, X turns off its B indicator.

Program X is interrupted at event 4. The input requires program Z, so Z's B indicator is turned on. In event 5, when the control program searches the table, Z appears as the highest priority unsuppressed program. Program X has a lower priority. Z gets control. It turns on its A indicator and turns off its B. Program Z is trapped in 6 by an input which is queued on Y. The right-hand column now shows the first Y input (item 1) in Y's queue. Control is returned to Z.

Event 7 is a trap requesting W. After W's B indicator is turned on, the control program returns control to Z at the instruction following the address where it was interrupted. A second input for Y (item 2) occurs in 8, after which Z is resumed. In event 9, program Z, having terminated, turns off its A indicator. Now Y, the present highest priority unsuppressed program, obtains control and turns on its A indicator. Program Y starts by removing input item 1 from the top of its queue. Y does not turn off its B indicator, because an item is still left in its input list. However, in event 10, Y finishes processing its first input. Still in control, Y removes the 2 input from its queue. Now Y turns off its B indicator. Event 11 shows Y terminating, at which point X resumes where it was interrupted previously.

Program X is completed in event 12. W is now the highest priority unsuppressed program. Upon obtaining control, W turns on its A indicator, and suppresses Z by turning on Z's C indicator. A third input for Y occurs in 13.

† My thanks to Gerald M. Weinberg for this illustration.

Event	Changes	Z A	Z B	Z C	Y A	Y B	Y C	X A	X B	X C	W A	W B	W C	Y's queue
1. Start of system	Processing in DIAG													
2. Trap	Requests X								X					
3. Enter X								X						
4. Trap	Requests Z		X					X						
5. Enter Z		X						X						
6. Trap	Requests Y—item 1, re-enter Z	X				X		X						1
7. Trap	Requests W, re-enter Z	X				X		X				X		1
8. Trap	Requests Y—item 2, re-enter Z	X				X		X				X		1, 2
9. Finish	$Z - - A$ off, enter Y, remove item 1 from queue				X	X		X				X		2
10. Finish $Y1$	Enter Y, remove item 2 from queue—B off					X		X				X		
11. Finish $Y2$	$Y - - A$ off, re-enter X at interrupt point							X				X		
12. Finish X	$X - - A$ off, enter W, suppress Z		X								X			
13. Trap	Requests Y—item 3		X		X						X			3
14. Trap from control program	Requests Z, enter Y—item 3		X	X	X						X			
15. Finish $Y3$	$Y - - A$ off, re-enter W		X	X							X			
16. Finish W	$W - - A$ off, $Z - - C$ off, enter Z	X												
17. Trap	Requests W, re-enter Z	X										X		
18. Finish Z	$Z - - A$ off, enter W, suppress Z		X									X		
19. Finish W	$W - - A$ off, $Z - - C$ off, enter DIAG													

The control program is interrupted in 14 while it is searching the table to decide what to do next. This input, a request for Z, causes Z's B indicator to be turned on. Since Z is suppressed, Y gets control. Program Y unqueues its input 3, turns off its B indicator, and turns on its A indicator. Y finishes in 15, turning off its A indicator. The control program gives control to W. Upon terminating in 16, W turns off its A indicator, and unsuppresses Z. Program Z now obtains control, turning its B off and its A on. An input at 17 is queued on W, after which Z is resumed.

Program Z finishes in event 18. It turns off its A indicator. Now W obtains control, and suppresses Z. In 19, W finishes, turning off its A. The diagnostic program DIAG now gets control, which it retains until the next input.

THE CONTROL PROGRAM

The priority table enables the computer to remember an entire stack of interrupts, and to keep track of a continually changing set of priority relationships among the operational programs. We have seen that the control program itself can be trapped. The priority program is a very short routine (less than 75 instructions), but since it is executed very frequently, the time taken for its executions has to be considered in the light of input requirements. If the control program ran with traps disabled, there would be a greater probability that information would not be moved out of filled core buffers fast enough to avoid the loss of data. If trapping were prevented while the control program was running, another interrupt would have to be remembered by the channel, and the interrupt subroutines would not have the opportunity to move the data out of the filled buffer immediately.

Another saving of time is made possible by not saving the contents of the registers used by the control program before it is interrupted. Since the control program always starts again from its first instruction after having been trapped, there is no need to save and later restore this information.

Each operational program is not completely responsible for all of the processing required by an input. In practice, one operational program may often call upon a successor program. When this occurs, the first program turns on the next program's B indicator, and enters its results in this next program's input queue.

It is possible for an operational program to call upon itself. In certain circumstances, a program may even suppress itself. Programmers must carefully study the implications of suppression, to avoid logical contradiction. For example, two programs may mutually suppress each other under such conditions that neither program can later be executed.

The basic loop of the Mercury control program is shown in Fig. 6-1.

Basic loop of control program

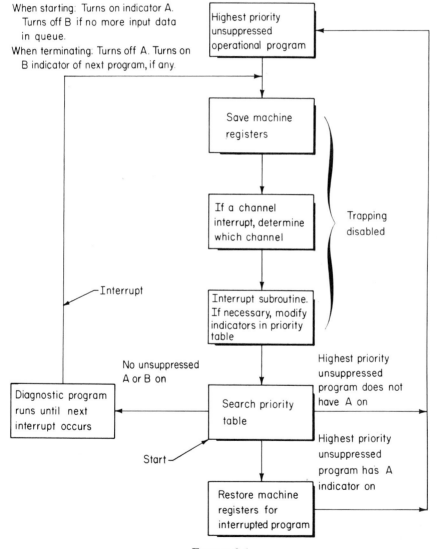

Figure 6-1

While input data is placed on a program's input queue, or when an item is removed from such a queue, interrupts are disabled. This is done for programming reasons. If an interrupt program sought to add an item to the list during queuing or unqueuing, the trap routine might interfere with the queuing or unqueuing programs, and information could be lost.

The decision procedure for removing entries from queues varies according to the program. The last-in, first-out method processes the last item entered on the list, whereas the first-in, first-out procedure picks the item which has been waiting for the longest time.

In Mercury, multiprogramming is used with tape operations. Certain communications to human controllers are made by messages transmitted to the printer. Since all possible printout messages cannot be kept in core, some messages are stored on tape. When a program decides to send a communication to the printer, it initiates a tape search for the desired message. If a second I/O operation were requested for this tape before the first search was complete, the computer would stall waiting for the termination of the first request. The CPU would remain idle until the I/O ended. To avoid this situation, whenever a program requests a tape search, it suppresses itself, then returns control to the control program.

Other programs now get control until an interrupt occurs, signaling completion of the tape operation. The message, with appropriate data entered into it, now is sent to the printer. At the termination of transmission to the printer, a second interrupt occurs. Only now can the search program be unsuppressed. The reason why the search program must remain suppressed during the printer operation is because the printer uses the same channel as the message tape. A second operation initiated on a channel before a prior operation is complete stalls the computer, making it idle until the first operation is finished.

As a general rule, an operation using a channel may not be initiated until the previous operation is complete. Hence, any program commencing transmission through a channel must suppress both itself and all other programs which might request an operation with that channel.

PROGRAM SPACE ALLOCATION

The computers used for the Mercury project have a 65K core memory. This memory is composed of upper core and lower core. Programs can be executed only in lower core. During the orbit phase (which requires the most computing) all of the operational programs cannot be kept in lower core. The more rarely used routines are hence kept in upper core. When they are needed, they are exchanged with a program now in lower core. The requested operational program has a preassigned area in lower core to which it is moved. Therefore, no program relocation is necessary; each program is compiled with its origin at the beginning of its preassigned core region. The program which formerly occupied this space is moved to upper memory, via a buffer, prior to bringing in the new program. The old program does not have to be initialized when it is later moved back into lower core. The programs which are exchanged are planned to be of approximately the same size.

It is true that the exchange of programs causes a delay. However, during the orbit phase sufficient time is available to absorb this lag without generating any problems.

The mechanics of initiating the movement of a program from upper core to lower core are as follows: When the Mercury machine is brought into operation, the entire programming system is initialized. If a given routine is loaded in upper core, a flag is placed in the program's entry in the priority table. This flag, called the R bit, has some similarity to the C indicator. The R bit signifies that the program cannot be entered, and that it is now in upper memory. At some point, the control program, upon searching the priority table, finds that the highest priority unsuppressed program has its R indicator on. The control program then gives control to a subroutine which moves this program into lower memory. After the requested program is in lower core, its R indicator is turned off. Now the control program can give control to this program when it reaches highest priority.

MULTIPLE REQUESTS FOR THE SAME PROGRAM

A running program may be interrupted by an input which is then placed on that program's input queue. Items may also be placed on a program's input queue by other routines which request the program.

The following question arises: Suppose a running program is interrupted by inputs with higher priorities. This program will hence not be able to resume until some time in the future. Assume that during this quiescent period the same program is requested by another input or another routine. Will not the second request interfere with the data already generated by the interrupted program? Will not the second request produce erroneous results because of dynamic modifications made in the program by the first request?

These problems do not occur in the Mercury system. The second request is not permitted to make use of the program until the program has finished processing the first input.

As we have seen, in the airline reservation systems, a later request *is* allowed to use an operational program, even if the previous request for that program is not processed completely. This is necessary in commercial applications where long delays often occur in programs while they await the completion of an I/O request. If a program could not be used during these stalled periods, the system would be slowed down, and the response time would be unduly increased.

In the Mercury system, an interrupt routine saves all of the CPU registers in special locations assigned to the interrupted program. Just before the program is given control to resume using the CPU, this information is restored. There is thus no loss of intermediate data. In the commercial applications we have been considering, the entry block technique is needed because one program may be used simultaneously by more than one input.

There are instances in Mercury when a number of different programs may refer to common information. Certain memory locations, called *communication cells*, are permanently reserved for such data.

THE GEMINI PROJECT

The real-time system being developed at the Goddard Space Flight Center for nonrendezvous Gemini will utilize the same monitor logic as was used for Mercury. Insofar as operational programs are concerned, numerous changes will be made in the mathematical routines. Because the Titan II booster will be employed instead of the Mercury Atlas, the launch programs will be altered considerably. Since Gemini will use a different re-entry technique from Mercury, the operational programs for this phase will be rewritten completely.

The system configuration at the Goddard Space Flight Center will be the same as was used for the last Mercury shot. This system included three 7094 computers, each with a 65K memory and an IBM 7281 data communication channel with 32 subchannels. As currently planned, two computers will run in parallel, but only one machine at a time is chosen to output.

A new system for rendezvous Gemini and for Apollo is under development in Houston, Texas.

7 ON-LINE COMPUTING CENTERS

THE PROBLEM OF TURN-AROUND TIME

The slow interaction between humans and computers has motivated the Massachusetts Institute of Technology and other computing centers to experiment with the time-sharing of computers by a number of users. The *turn-around* time required to receive outputs after a program is submitted to a computer is often several hours, or even a couple of days. This delay is often excessive for research and development programs. A reduction in turn-around time would not only benefit such projects, but also would probably attract additional scientists and engineers to computation centers.

Similar advantages would result from the decrease in the time required to debug programs. It is impractical to let a programmer test his program by sitting at the console of a large machine. Hence, debugging must be carried on through the same automatic system as is used for production runs. The correction of programming errors may drag on for a relatively long time, since a minor mistake may necessitate another turn-around period.

A system is needed in which several programmers can have immediate access to the computer simultaneously. Such an installation would enable users to obtain their outputs more rapidly, and would provide for on-line debugging.

What has been proposed is a multiconsole computing center.† Each user would be able to enter a program at any time from his terminal,

† As stated previously, this book does not treat multiple-computer systems.

and communicate with the computer whenever necessary. In actuality, each program would be run for a short period of time, perhaps a few milliseconds, after which the next program would have its turn. However, the high speed of the machine and the slowness of human reactions would give each user the equivalent of a computer entirely at his immediate command.

Such a time-sharing system would have the additional value of enabling the user to direct the computer to take appropriate program branches as the result of intermediate results in the computation. At present, all decision points in programs must be specified completely in advance. If the user were in virtually continuous communication with the machine, he could immediately give the computer branching directives after receiving the results thus far of the calculation. This procedure would make it easier for mathematicians, engineers, and scientists to work creatively with the computer in exploring the effects of different parameters or functions.

Another potential value of multiconsole systems might lie in their adaptability for use as teaching machines. Every student would be able to follow a programmed course of instruction at his own rate, the computer providing such displays and messages as were necessary for each person.

Many advanced methods for man-computer communication have been suggested for time-sharing systems. With special consoles, users could prepare graphic inputs which would be recognized and analyzed by the computer. Outputs could be displayed in graphic form.

A possible configuration for an on-line debugging system could include IBM 1014 remote inquiry units. These devices are Selectric typewriters which transmit information to the central processor through an 80-character buffer in a 1414 VI input-output synchronizer. The user signals the processor when an 80-character (or less) line has been completed by means of the Selectric's "carriage-return" key. When this key is depressed, the information which has just been typed is sent to the buffer; the processor empties the buffer by a special command. It is possible for a user to delete a message in the buffer before the carriage-return key is depressed. In an on-line system, the computer would probably empty the buffer before the carriage had been mechanically returned, so the user would not be aware of any delay in communicating with the machine. The input-output synchronizer has sufficient buffering for handling three 1014 units at a time.

STORAGE ALLOCATION

The allocation of core storage to the users' programs generates numerous difficulties. If a 32K 7090 were used, perhaps 8000 words would be used by the control program. This area would include input-output regions as well as space for instructions. Hence, if six terminals were in the system, only about 4000 words would be available for each user's program.

The smaller the amount of core available to each terminal, the more restricted each programmer would be. The programmer would be forced to store parts of his program externally, bringing in extra sections when necessary. Furthermore, if only a small amount of core were available to each programmer, there would be a frequent moving in and out of programs. The greater the time taken by input-output, the slower the entire system would be. Hence, the larger the number of users' areas main memory is divided into, the more are the restrictions placed on the programmer and the less efficient is the working of the system.

Enough programs must be in core at one time to permit multiprogramming to occur (to have available another program to receive control while one or more of the others are awaiting the completion of input-output requests). Hence, a compromise must be reached between the advantage of multiprogramming and the disadvantage of frequent input-output of programs. If three programs were kept in memory at the same time, each could use 8000 words. This allocation might not restrict the programmer unduly; at the same time, it might make possible a high degree of multiprogramming overlapping.

Memory protection is particularly vital in an on-line debugging system, where untested programs might frequently injure other programs in memory at the same time. Trapping of input-output requests is also necessary, in order to restrict reading and writing to the proper areas in memory, and to facilitate multiprogramming under the authority of the control program. The control program also makes sure that programs write information only into their assigned areas in disks, tapes, and terminals.

Program relocation is necessary in a time-sharing system where a number of consoles can be on-line simultaneously. Since users' programs are continually moved in and out of memory, a program may be executed from any available area in memory. Hence, a technique is necessary for incrementing instructions so as to execute them from any part of core storage.

Although users' programs would usually be of different sizes, it probably would be undesirable to allot variable size core areas to each program. It would be possible for the control program to keep an available storage list, and to allocate parts of core to each program as these memory areas became usable. The difficulty with this approach is that the available core storage would probably become noncontiguous. As we explained on page 41, this would result in the fragmentation of programs into two or more parts.

Here, in Fig. 7-1, is an example of what might happen if the control program were to bring in a user's program as soon as there was enough room for it in memory.

In phase (1) of the memory layout depicted below (control program not shown), programs 1 and 2 are in core, leaving a small amount of memory available. Now program 1 finishes its allotted time. It is written out by the control program, which reads in program 3. However, 3 requires more than the space formerly allotted to 1. Accordingly, 3 is broken up into two sections in phase (2). In phase (3), program 4 is brought in after 2 is written out. There is now room for program 5, but it must be broken into two parts as shown in phase (4).

Since programs would be written out and read in every few milliseconds as they finished their allotted time, there would be a tendency for memory to become increasingly chopped up. This would not only cause bookkeeping and control problems, but would make it difficult

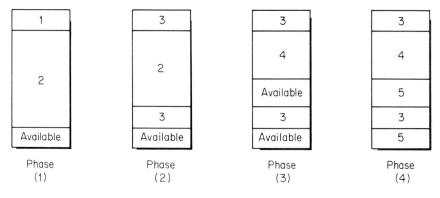

FIGURE 7-1

to devise satisfactory memory protection and program relocation schemes. Possibly the technique suggested on pages 42-44 might be employed advantageously here. One way to avoid the scattering of programs into noncontiguous parts of memory would be to allot standard-size blocks to each program.

SYSTEM CONFIGURATION

Because programs are continually being moved in and out by the control program, they must be stored in a random-access unit. Furthermore, users must be able to request the execution of any of their programs. For fast service, therefore, all programs must be stored in a random-access device. In addition, various utility programs, such as compilers, memory prints, and tracers, are needed by users, who must

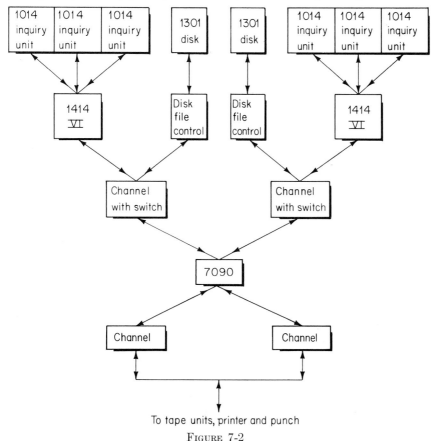

To tape units, printer and punch

FIGURE 7-2

be able to call upon these programs without being subjected to delay. Because of the limited number of tape units available for sharing among several users, it is desirable to provide users with another type of bulk storage. This backup memory must be fast enough to avoid slowing up the system with numerous long input-output requests. For our hypothetical system, let us assume that two 1301 disk files are employed for these purposes.

It is possible for the 1414 VI to share a channel with a 1301 disk file. A programmable switch enables the computer to switch the channel to either unit. The 1014 terminals do not use an appreciable amount of channel time. A person typing at the fast rate of 12.5 characters per second would type in 75 characters in 6 seconds. However, it takes only about 40 milliseconds of channel time to empty a 1414 VI buffer into the 7090.

An on-line computing center with six 1014 terminals, two disk files, and other conventional equipment might appear as shown in Fig. 7-2.

A clock is necessary in the main computer to interrupt the machine at specified intervals. This is necessary to limit the amount of time used by each user program, and to guard against endless loops in the programs being debugged.

THE CONTROL PROGRAM

The control program must maintain a CPU queue, on which is kept a list of all users' programs waiting for an opportunity to be executed. If just one of the six terminals is active, control will be given to this program after each timing interrupt. However, if more than one program is running, another program may be ready for CPU time, in which case it will be on the CPU queue.

Even if more than one user is active, all of the programs may not be ready for CPU time. One reason for this is that a given program may still be waiting for the completion of an input-output request; only when this request has been completed will the control program place the program on the CPU list. In addition, if six programs are being run simultaneously, there will not be room in core for all of them at the same time. Hence, programs not in core at a particular time will not be on the CPU list.

To provide an equitable use of CPU time and to avoid causing users to wait unduly for a response from the computer, a modified round-robin approach must be employed.

Let us assume that the core available for users' programs is divided into three parts, each section being available for one program. Hence, only three out of the six programs can simultaneously be in memory. Now suppose that four users request execution of their programs. As each user makes an execution request, the control program attaches a number to his program. The programs would be numbered 1, 2, 3, and 4 (these numbers are not related to the terminals, but are based on the order in which the programs are requested). The basic procedure in the control program is to give priority to each of these programs in turn, starting with 1, and ending with program 4. After 4 has been executed, the control program gives priority to 1 once more, and the process is repeated. The program with priority is the program to which control is given, i.e., it is the program which is executed now by the CPU. After a given program has used up its allotted time, it is placed at the bottom of the CPU list. If each program is permitted to run for 2 seconds, then, with four users active, each program is guaranteed access to the CPU at least once every 8 seconds.

The priority program is at the top of the CPU queue for 2 seconds. Of course, during the time it has control, it may temporarily lose control of the CPU when it makes an input-output request. But the program regains control when this I/O request is complete. It retains priority until its allotted 2 seconds expire.

When a program makes an input-output request, it yields control. The control program now consults the CPU queue. If there is another program in memory which can use the CPU, this program is on the CPU queue, and the control program gives it control. This second program retains control until the priority program's input-output request has been completed, at which point the computer is interrupted, and the control program returns control to the priority program.

REPLACEMENT ALGORITHM

There are several ways in which programs in core can be replaced by other programs. With four or more programs active, there are frequent occasions when another program must be read in to take its turn as priority program. Since users' programs may be self-modified as they run, they must be saved until they are executed again. Users' programs cannot simply be overwritten by another program. Before a program now stored on the disk can be read in, the program presently in core must be written out. So that replacement involves always the output of 8000 words of core and the input of 8000 words of core. Even though these programs are stored in rapid-access portions of the disks, these input-output times constitute a major factor in disk usage, and slow up the users' programs' disk requests. Hence, a technique is needed which minimizes the time required for the input-output of programs.

One way of interchanging programs would simply be always to write out the program which has just lost priority, and to bring in the program now on the disk. Thus, if 1, 2, and 3 were now in core, and 2 were just completed, then 2 would be written out, and 4 read in. While this was occurring, 3 would be executed. As soon as 3 finished its allotted time, it would be written out, and 2 read in while 4 was running. With this method, an interchange would occur after each program lost priority. Every 2 seconds the channel would be occupied for a substantial amount of time while the interchange occurred.

Another method is to interchange when the successor program to the program which has just received priority is not in core. For example, if 1, 2, and 3 are now in core, and 1 finishes its allotted time, then 2 is ready to receive priority. Since the successor to 2, namely 3, is in core, no interchange occurs. However, when 2 is finished, and 3 receives priority, the control program notes that the successor to 3, namely 4, is not in core. At this moment, the program just completed (2) is written out, and 4 is read in. The interchange is always between the successor and predecessor of the program just receiving priority. Here is a diagram depicting this interchange algorithm. The circled number indicates the program which has just received priority and is about to obtain control from the control program.

Elapsed time (seconds)	0–2	2–4	4–6	6–8	8–10	10–12	12–14
	①	1	1	1	①	1	1
	2	②	4→2	④	2→4	②	4→2
	3	3	③	3	3	3	③

At the start, programs 1, 2, and 3 are in core. Program 1 is about to receive control. Its successor, 2, is in core, so the control program does not initiate an interchange.

At the end of 2 seconds, 1 loses control and 2 receives priority. Program 2's successor (3) is in core, so no interchange occurs.

At the end of 4 seconds, 2 loses control and 3 becomes the priority program. Since 3's successor (4) is not in memory, the control program initiates an interchange by writing out 3's predecessor (2), and reading in 4. By the way, there is ample time to perform the interchange within the 2 seconds while 3 is running. Hence, when 3 is finished, program 4 is in core and ready to run. Since 4's successor (1) is in core, no interchange is necessary at this time.

In this method, an interchange occurs 50% of the time, for once the initial condition has been passed there is an interchange at the beginning of every alternate timing interval. If five programs are active, interchanges occur only $33\frac{1}{3}$% of the time.

In practice, the actual amount of time a program retains priority might often be more than its allotted 2 seconds. This occurs whenever the priority program makes an input-output request. During this time, this program loses control of the CPU. Presumably, the user would not be charged for this time, and the control program would not log this program for CPU time while it was awaiting the completion of an input-output request. Hence, the above description of the replacement algorithm is somewhat oversimplified. However, the principle remains as stated.

Various sophistications can be added to the algorithm to make it more efficient. For example, it will be noted that with four programs running, programs 1 and 3 always remain in core, while 2 and 4 are the only programs interchanged. This does not affect the amount of time taken for interchanges. However, an inequity does result for programs 2 and 4. While a program is in core, it will always be on the CPU list, unless it is awaiting the completion of a disk or tape request. Since programs 2 and 4 are in core less often than 1 and 3, the former pair of programs lose out on extra CPU time they might acquire. Hence, it will take them longer to be completed. This situation can easily be remedied by alternating the procedure periodically, so that the pair being interchanged is switched with the pair remaining in memory. Another technique is to credit the CPU time obtained by a nonpriority program toward its next allotted time period.

A disk request queue and a tape request queue are maintained by the control program. Whenever a request is completed, the requesting program is returned to the CPU queue. If the requesting program is the program with priority, the currently running program is interrupted, and control is returned to the priority program. Whenever the priority program makes a disk request, the amount of its allocated time it has already spent is stored by the control program, and is restored when the priority program regains control. If this were not done, the priority program would be logged for time it spent while not using the CPU.

OTHER FUNCTIONS OF THE MONITOR

Before any interchange of programs is initiated by the control program, the control program checks to make sure that the program about to be written out has not made an input-output request which is still pending. If an interchange were initiated while such a request were pending, confusion would result. For example, suppose program 2 made a disk request. This would be placed on the disk request queue. Assume now that 2 is to be interchanged with program 4, and that 2 is indeed written out. When program 2's request is executed, it will be read into a core area now occupied by 4.

A number of other functions are performed by the control program. As has been stated, a log is kept of the amount of time spent by each of the users' programs. The accounting procedure might take into consideration, not merely the CPU time employed by a program, but also the time required for tape and disk requests, the number of tapes used, and the amount of disk storage employed. The control program would decide how to allocate the tape units to users. Since a limited number of tape units are available, the users may be asked to comply with rules governing the number of tape units they are permitted to employ.

MAN-MACHINE COMMUNICATION

The control program will probably send a message to a console if that user's program is exceeding its estimated time by too great an interval. This communication enables the user to decide whether his program is caught in an endless loop. The users will have available instructions for requesting the computer to perform numerous functions.

For example, the user will be able to request compilations, program executions, and the employment of various debugging aids, such as selected printouts on the typewriter. The individual at the console will have some way of identifying himself and his programs. He will need to insert, delete, and correct instructions and data. The user should have the capacity to terminate the execution of a program or to end outputting of information on his typewriter. A large part of the control program will probably consist of subprograms for communicating with the consoles and for carrying out users' directives. The programmer will be able to request compilation of programs written in FORTRAN and other such languages.

8 THE PROGRAMMED TRANSMISSION CONTROL

CONNECTING A COMPUTER TO TERMINALS

Numerous problems arise in linking a central data processor to a network of terminals through real-time communication lines. Many techniques must be developed to manage the real-time relationship between the computer and its environment. Some of the major problems are as follows:

(1) All of the communication channels require input, output, and work areas. Incoming messages must be stacked somewhere in storage, and output messages from the central processor must be queued prior to transmission. Temporary areas are required for preliminary processing of incoming and outgoing messages. Sufficient memory must be available to enable the machine to store all inputs and outputs waiting to be handled, yet excessive memory must not be used. Since the volume of input-output cannot be predicted in advance, the storage allocated for these purposes must be capable of expanding and contracting as conditions from time to time demand. Special list structure programs are needed for allocating storage.

(2) The code which is used by the terminals is often different from the machine code. Therefore, a conversion from machine language to the terminal's code is frequently necessary when a message is to be outputted, and vice-versa when an input message is received.

(3) The validity of input characters must be checked by the generation of input check characters. In addition, faulty components in the communication network must be detected, isolated, and corrected.

(4) Control must be exercised over the remote terminals to prevent them from overloading the processor during peak periods. The machine may not be able to handle the interrupts fast enough, or its memory may not be able to contain all of the input messages. Hence, some way of shutting off the transmission of inputs from the terminals is desirable. In some systems, it is necessary to give priority to messages from certain terminals.

(5) The physical equipment linking the processor to the communication lines must enable different types of messages to be received or outputted. A central computer may be linked to such equipment as telegraph machines, punched-card transmitters and receivers, and magnetic tape transmitters and receivers. Each of these devices uses different codes and has different transmission rates. A physical interface is needed between the central processor and every type of input-output unit.

THE PROGRAMMED TRANSMISSION CONTROL

By performing these functions, the Programmed Transmission Control (IBM 7750)† frees the central computer for data processing activities. This machine, the PTC, receives all inputs and transmits all outputs. It assembles, edits, converts, and prepares all input-output messages with its own stored programs, and at the same time accepts directions from the main processor. Since the PTC can also switch messages from one part of a communication network to another, it is able to relieve the central computer of this burden.

One large system will include three 7750's. One unit handles transactions while another processes operational and administrative teletype traffic. The third Programmed Transmission Control backs up others in the event of a temporary machine failure. The Sabre data channels are adequate for American Airlines, since that system receives only high-speed inputs. But where input-output messages are transmitted at various speeds, 7750's are necessary.

---

† The 7740, a later version of the 7750, performs substantially the same functions as the 7750.

An additional advantage of the PTC is that it provides more buffering of inputs. Hence, the central processor is less likely to become overloaded.

The PTC provides an interface between any type of central data processing unit and any type of terminal. For example, either a 1410, 7040, 7080, or 7090 can be connected to a communications network by the PTC. Hence, the designer of a real-time system is able to choose a central computer without being concerned about how the processor will be connected to the remote terminals.

The 7750 assembles incoming bits from the terminals into messages, stores this information in its own memory, performs preliminary processing of the messages, and transmits this data to the main computer. The PTC carries out similar functions on information from the processor destined for remote transmission. By monitoring the input messages, the PTC maintains an image of the communication network, and controls the rate of input from the terminals by means of its stored programs. Transmission of data to and from the computer occurs at the rate of about 70,000 characters per second.

CONTROL STORAGE AND PROCESS STORAGE

There are two major components of the PTC, each of which operates autonomously, with its own memory unit. Both components provide each other with input-output and control information. The functional unit called *control storage* performs the automatic operations associated with the assembly of input messages and the distribution of output messages. The other unit, *process storage*, processes messages, communicates with the main computer, and operates under the control of programs stored in its own memory. The overall flow of information in the PTC is shown in Fig. 8-1.

ASSEMBLY OF BITS IN CHANNEL WORDS

As bits arrive from the input channels, they are placed into *channel words* in control storage. Control storage contains 128 words of 48 bits each. Each channel is assigned a particular control word. As each bit arrives from a channel and is placed in its channel word, the channel word is automatically shifted one bit position. When the last bit position of a character is filled, the entire character is transferred

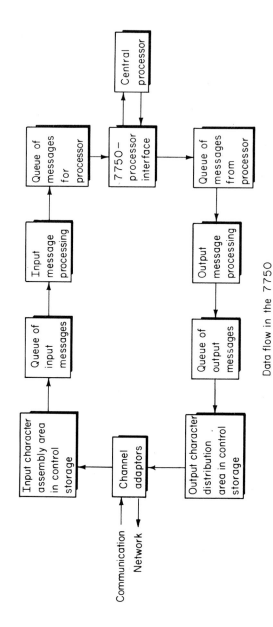

Data flow in the 7750

Figure 8-1

92

automatically into process storage. It is in process storage that code conversions, format changes, editing, and other operations take place by means of stored programs.

Output messages from the main computer are held in process storage. Each character in turn is transferred automatically into control storage. Here the character is distributed into bits, which are transmitted to the proper terminal.

As has been stated, each channel word in control storage is associated with a communication line. In the case of high-speed channels, however, three or four words of control storage may be needed. One of these words holds data; the others are used for control purposes. Communication channels are attached to the PTC through channel adaptors, which enable both high- and low-speed inputs to enter the 7750. In the usual case, 11 bits of the channel word are reserved for bits of incoming or outgoing characters. All 11 bit positions, however, need not be used. The channel word normally contains several control fields for regulating input and output. These control fields are stored in the channel word by the program, which can modify the fields when necessary.

TRANSFER OF CHARACTERS TO PROCESS STORAGE

After an input character of 11 or less bits has been assembled in the control word, there is an automatic interrupt of the program under way in process storage. The completed character is placed in a preassigned location in process storage. Output characters are moved from process storage to control storage in a similar fashion.

Process storage locations are assigned to incoming messages in the following manner: The areas reserved for messages are composed of eight-word blocks. Each word contains space for four characters. Thus, there are 32 character positions in each block. However, the last character position is used for a pointer character, in case the given block has to be chained to another similar block. Each character in a block has a 16-bit address, consisting of a 11-bit block address, followed by a three-bit word address and a two-bit character address. Any eight words in process storage can serve as a block so long as the address of the first word is 00. Figure 8-2 is an example of a block in process storage. Its address (octal) is 123.

The two-bit character address for each word runs from 00 to 11

Block address⟋ ⌐Word address
        ⌐Character address

00 001 010 011 |000|00 Character of 11 bits or less	00 001 010 011 |000|01		00 001 010 011 |000|11
– – – –	– – – –	– – – –	– – – –
00 001 010 011 |001|00	– – – –	– – – –	– – – –
– – – –	– – – –	– – – –	– – – –
– – – –	– – – –	– – – –	– – – –
– – – –	– – – –	– – – –	– – – –
– – – –	– – – –	– – – –	– – – –
– – – –	– – – –	– – – –	– – – –
– – – –	– – – –	– – – –	– – – –
– – – –	– – – –	– – – –	– – – –
– – – –	– – – –	– – – –	– – – –
– – – –	– – – –	– – – –	– – – –
00 001 010 011 |011|00	– – – –	– – – –	00 001 010 011 |011|11
– – – –	– – – –	– – – –	– – – –
00 001 010 011 |111|00	– – – –	– – – –	00 001 010 011 |111|11
– – – –	– – – –	– – – –	Address of next block in the chain

FIGURE 8-2

for the four characters. The word address starts at 000 for the first word, and ends at 111 for the seventh word in the block. The 11-bit block address remains the same for every word in the entire block. Therefore, the low-order five bits of the first character in a block always consist of 00000, and the low-order five bits of the last character position always end with 11111. This enables the end-of-block condition to be recognized automatically by control storage.

Before the transmission of an input message is initiated, the program places the address of the first character in the block into the appropriate channel word. After the bits constituting the first character of the message have been assembled and transferred to the first character position in the assigned block in process storage, the address in the channel word is automatically incremented by 1. This causes the second assembled character to be placed in the second character position of the block. In this way, each character of a message is placed sequentially in its proper position in process storage. After the 31st character has been transferred into process storage, the address in the channel word is stepped by 1 again, thereby causing the last five characters to be 11111. Upon recognizing this condition, control storage automatically requests a special program which assigns the next block of process storage to this continuing message. The address of the first character position in this next block is placed by the program into the channel word. Now the automatic input procedure is re-initiated. The 32nd character of the input message, when assembled, is transferred into the first character of the newly chained block.

PROCESS STORAGE

Process storage may consist of 4096, 8192, or 16,384 words of 48 bits. These words may be used either for data, instructions, or for chaining control:

(1) When used for holding data, words consist of four 11-bit fields, each of which can contain a character composed of as many as 11 bits. Characters consisting of less than 11 bits are stored in the low-order bit positions; the unused positions are set to zero.

(2) PTC instructions have a single address. An instruction word contains an address field, an operation code, and two flag bits. In addition, the instruction word has four other fields, used for specifying registers and fields employed in address modification and data processing.

(3) The chain control, or *limit* word, contains the address of the first character in a chain, as well as the address of the last character in a chain. It also has a field which can be used as a counter of the number of blocks in a chain.

The machine cycle of the PTC is 28 microseconds. Certain instructions require two machine cycles. There is no arithmetic unit in the 7750, so that all arithmetic operations, as well as shifts and comparisons, must be accomplished by means of lookups in stored tables. The instruction set provides for indirect addressing, to facilitate the handling of messages chained in blocks. An assembly program which runs on the 1401 produces a PTC program which can be loaded into process storage via the 1410 or 7000 series machines.

Since messages in a real-time system enter at random and have a random length, it cannot be predicted in advance when the PTC will have to receive or send information to the communication lines. As a consequence, it also cannot be ascertained beforehand when the various PTC programs will be called upon to process these messages, and how long these programs will have to run to handle the messages. Finally, certain types of processing are of greater urgency than others, and it is impossible to know when the programs associated with these problems will be needed. Hence, a priority system is required to enable the PTC to turn its attention, when necessary, to events of more importance. This is achieved by an interrupt feature which causes the machine to switch automatically from a currently running program to one of higher priority.

PROGRAM MODES

The PTC can run in any of six program modes. Here are these modes, in order of high-to-low priority:

(1) *Service mode* is chiefly used to detect communication errors. The mode is initiated either manually by the operator, automatically upon the occurrence of an error, or upon request of a program. The PTC enters this mode if a check switch on the operator's panel is turned on; otherwise the machine stops. The service mode is also used for debugging, engineering diagnostics, and for preparing error messages.

(2) *Channel service mode* is automatically requested when some multiple of the first 31 characters of an input or output message has been transferred from control storage to process storage, or vice-versa. The program which runs in this mode keeps track of available blocks—it maintains a list of free blocks which can be used for additional storage. When the channel service mode is requested after an input block has been filled with 31 characters, the program assigns a free block to the continuing input message. The address of this next block is stored in the channel word for that communication line. When 31 characters from a block containing an output message have been transferred to

control storage, the PTC automatically requests the channel service mode. In this case, the program gives the channel word the address of the next block in the chain, and returns the freed block to the available block list.

(3) *Copy mode* is executed automatically; a stored program is not used to carry out its functions. When the machine is in this mode, it transfers data to or from the main processor. The PTC enters copy mode upon the request of some program.

(4) *Out mode* is used to set up a control word which prepares the copy mode to transmit information to the main processor. This control word, called the *copy mode process word*, informs the PTC how and where to move the data. The out mode is usually requested by the main computer; it is turned off by the 7750. The PTC may itself request the out mode. The out mode requests the copy mode.

(5) *In mode* sets up a copy mode process word which is used by the copy mode for transmitting data from the central computer to the PTC. This program ascertains where space is available for the message in process storage, and it requests the copy mode. The in mode is usually requested by a program in the main processor, and is turned off by the PTC program.

(6) *Normal mode,* which has the lowest priority, performs all of the other programmed functions of the 7750, such as error checking, translation of codes, recognition of special characters, supervision of the communication network, and queuing of messages.

EXECUTION OF THE MODES

The mode in which the PTC operates is determined by the mode request register and the mode status register. These are five-bit registers, each of the bit positions representing one of the modes. The absence of any bits represents the normal mode.

When a mode is requested, the corresponding bit is turned on in the mode request register, which is addressable by a program. If more than one mode is requested over a period of time, the PTC selects the requested mode which has the highest priority. The mode selected is turned on in the mode status register. This register, which is not addressable by a program, contains at most one bit at a time. The bit which is present automatically causes the machine to enter the designated mode. As has been stated, if no bits are on in the mode status register, the PTC enters the normal mode.

Each mode has a process word in control storage. This word contains an instruction counter and fields which can be used as addressable registers for data manipulation. With the exception of the copy mode, the process words control the sequence of operations in each of the modes.

When a mode is selected, the process word corresponding to that mode is made available, and its instruction counter determines what instruction in that mode is to be executed next. When a program in a certain mode is interrupted by a request for a higher priority mode, the process word of the new mode is automatically selected, and the machine proceeds to carry out the instruction specified in the new mode's instruction counter. Since each mode has its own process word, there is no need to save the contents of the registers and the instruction counter when a mode is interrupted. After a given mode has been completed, the PTC enters the next requested mode which has the highest priority. If a previously interrupted mode is now the highest priority requested mode, the 7750 continues with its program where it left off in the past.

A programmer can prevent mode interruption by tagging instructions. This procedure is followed when a certain operation must be completed without interruption.

CONTROL OF THE COMMUNICATION NETWORK

The communication channels attached to the PTC are either *half duplex* or *full duplex*. A half-duplex channel can be used either to send out or to receive information, but only one type of transmission can occur at a time: inputting and outputting cannot occur simultaneously. A full-duplex channel enables messages to be received and transmitted concomitantly.

A number of terminals may share one communication channel. This possibility gives a real-time system much greater capacity. However, where more than one terminal is connected to a channel, some technique is necessary to decide when each terminal will have access to the channel. The PTC makes this decision by *polling*. This procedure consists of sending a permissive signal to a terminal, enabling it to transmit over a channel. Since a terminal cannot use a channel until it receives permission, the 7750 is able to control the load on the entire system through polling. If the load becomes too heavy because of excessive inputs, the PTC can decrease polling and increase the output rate. Polling is used both on half-duplex and full-duplex channels.

When the input line of a full-duplex channel becomes available for transmission, it is necessary to poll the terminal from which the PTC next wishes to receive messages. If the outgoing channel is in use, how can the polling signal be transmitted? Must the 7750 wait until the message currently being outputted is completely transmitted?

It is instructive to consider the technique used to avoid such a wait. The characters comprising a polling message are placed at the end of some storage block. This is done when the constants used in the various programs are initially loaded in process storage. When polling becomes necessary, the program changes the address in the control word for that channel. It replaces the address of the next character to be outputted with the address of the first character in the polling message. As a result, after the last bit of the character currently being outputted is transmitted, the channel word obtains the first polling character, and transmits this message in the usual way.

Since the polling message is at the end of a block, control storage automatically requests channel service mode after this message has been completed. The program in the channel service mode places the address of the next character of the original message into the channel word. The PTC now continues to output this information. The block containing the polling message is not returned to the available storage list. Since it may be used again and again for the same purpose, it is retained as a constant in process storage.

TRANSMISSION DELAY

Messages sent from the main processor may contain various special characters, such as the carriage return symbol, which create some desired format when printed at the terminal. In such instances, it may be necessary for the PTC to insert a sending delay character between a format character and the following data character. This function is performed by a 7750 program which examines the message after it has been transferred into process storage from the computer. The sending delay character is followed by a number specifying the length of the desired delay. When the message containing the delay character is entered into the channel word, the machine automatically causes this delay to occur.

The delay is reckoned in terms of bit-times. A bit-time is the length of time it takes the PTC to send one bit to a terminal via a particular channel. A sending delay character requesting a delay of 750 bit-times on a 75-bit-per-second channel would produce a delay of 10 seconds. The maximum delay which can be requested is 2045 bit-times.

The transmission delay is also used when the PTC wants to send part of a message, and then wait for a specified length of time for an answer from the remote terminal. It is also possible for the 7750 to insert a status change character at the end of a message, followed by a delay count. Upon receiving the status change character, the line is immediately switched so that the PTC is able to listen for an antici-pated response.

PROGRAMMING THE PTC

As has been stated, the 7750 was developed to relieve the main processor of many communication functions not directly related to the major data processing activities required in the system. In planning an actual system, it is often the case that a certain procedure may be carried out either by the central computer or by the PTC. Of course, in some instances, the main processor must be assigned a particular function because it is faster or because it has access to the files. On the other hand, where the 7750 has special design characteristics, the PTC is given the task of carrying out a given procedure.

Where a function can be performed by both the PTC and the cen-tral processor, the choice depends on such factors as availability of storage in the machines, how much time the function would take in each, the speed or special instructions required for the processing, the efficiency with which the machines perform the activity, and the extent to which the assignment of the function provides for flexibility in the possible future expansion of the entire system. Programming convenience is of relatively minor significance in making the decision as to which machine will carry out the function.

Many of these factors cannot be accurately evaluated while a system is being developed, and the decision must often be based on estimates or incomplete information. Hence, it may be necessary to change a decision, if possible, after the system has crystallized.

USE OF PROGRAM MODES

The program executed while the PTC is in a given mode depends upon the address in that mode's instruction counter. As we have seen, each of the modes was intended for certain purposes by the designers. However, a programmer is at liberty to perform a procedure in any other mode he deems desirable. He may do so for various reasons. For example, the programmer may wish to take advantage of the higher priority of another mode. Or he may assign part of a particular function to the normal mode in order to shorten the time required to process that function in a higher priority mode.

The types of programs executed in the normal mode of course vary with the application. Some of the normal-mode functions are:

(1) Message header processing
(2) Message accounting
(3) Code conversion
(4) Checking the validity of characters
(5) Generation and comparison of redundancy check characters
(6) Editing, adding or deleting special control characters, and altering the message format
(7) Queuing input and output messages from the terminals and from the main processor
(8) Polling and allocating communication channels to terminals for incoming messages
(9) Initiating incoming and outgoing transmission
(10) Maintaining a list of available storage blocks, and checking to make sure that a minimum number of blocks are ready for use
(11) Keeping track of the status of channels and terminals
(12) Real-time diagnostic testing of malfunctioning network components
(13) Rerouting traffic away from malfunctioning components
(14) Communication with the humans operating the system
(15) Initiating communication with the main computer by means of an interrupt signal.

SERVICING THE TERMINALS

The basic function of the PTC is to maintain a well-balanced message flow between the terminals and the main processor. The time taken by the system to respond to inputs from different terminals should not be disproportionate (unless this is a specification of the application). Therefore, if the response time to inputs from all terminals is required to be about the same, it would be undesirable if the system design caused certain messages to be delayed unduly. Since most of the programmed processing in the 7750 occurs in the normal mode, the way in which normal-mode programs are planned exerts an important influence on the efficiency of the entire machine system.

The circuitry of the PTC provides, in effect, for simultaneous transmission on all of the communication lines. The communication channels are automatically scanned on schedule to provide for the receiving or sending of bits from the terminals.

The normal mode must be executed on a somewhat similar scanning schedule to avoid providing unequal service for the channels. It will be recalled that each message queued in the PTC is maintained in one or more chained blocks. Apart from applications involving message switching between terminals, such data consist of:

(1) Input messages from terminals waiting for preliminary processing in the PTC

(2) Input messages from terminals waiting to be transferred to the main computer after preliminary processing in the PTC

(3) Output messages from the main computer waiting for pretransmission processing in the PTC

(4) Output messages from the main computer waiting for transmission to terminals after having been prepared for outputting by the PTC.

Although the blocks allocated for these messages are assigned dynamically, each message area is associated with a particular communication channel. Every message must undergo some processing by the 7750 in the normal mode. However, if the normal mode waited until all of the characters comprising a message were in process storage, a relatively large amount of processing would then be required, and the response to the transaction would be delayed. Hence, the normal mode goes from message area to message area, in sequence, handling whatever characters have arrived. This scanning is repeated continually. As part of this procedure, the PTC checks the output message areas. If complete messages are ready for transmission, and the communication channel is available, the program initiates the output.

Programmers must estimate how much time they can allot for processing the new characters in one communication channel's area without building up undue delays in handling other channels' messages. The amount of time the normal-mode program can spend in processing one area must be limited by the programmer, to enable attention to be paid sufficiently soon to other areas in the scan.

For example, at the end of each message there are one or more end-of-message characters which signify that transmission is completed. When the program detects these characters in the input area of a half-duplex channel, the program has several operations to carry out: The message must be moved to a queue awaiting transmission to the main processor. One or more blocks must be returned to the available storage list. Finally, the output area for the channel must be examined: if a complete message is ready to be outputted, output on the channel must be initiated. The problem which arises is that, if the normal-mode program performs all of these functions at this time, the scan and processing of the succeeding areas will be delayed. For this reason, the programmer may plan to carry out only some of these procedures at this time. Indeed, the program may be scheduled not to execute any activities at all at this moment.

The programmer may plan so that the amount of processing performed at any given time depends upon how much processing of other areas is pending. In this way a flexible schedule can be maintained. It may also be necessary to give the program the capacity to change its schedule of scanning message areas in the event of load changes on the system over a period of time.

Priorities may be assigned to certain channels' areas in the scan. In such cases, the programmer decides the sequence in which message areas are scanned. Some areas may be allotted more time for servicing than others. The programmer devises a subroutine for determining the scanning sequence and allotting time for each channel's area.

Since any of the programs used within each of the modes may be called for at any time, all of these programs must be kept in process storage at all times. To provide as much storage as possible for the buffering of messages, it is important to keep these programs as short as feasible. The throughput of the PTC obviously should be kept as high as possible; this rate is influenced by the amount of buffer storage available.

COMMUNICATION WITH THE PROCESSOR

Special inquiries from terminals to the main processor can be handled as follows: When a terminal makes such an inquiry, the PTC interrupts the computer. After the processor replies, the 7750 transmits the message to the computer's core storage. The answer sent from the processor to the PTC is placed in process storage, where it is prepared for transmission back to the terminal. If this reply has a priority, it is placed at the head of the output queue for messages to that terminal.

Data are moved between the PTC and the main processor under the control of the copy mode process word, which recognizes the end-of-block condition in a fashion similar to the channel control words. The copy mode process word is incremented by one as each character is transferred. When its low-order five-bit positions consist of all ones, the pointer field at the end of the block is moved automatically into the copy mode process word, replacing the address of the completed block. Now the successor character is obtained from the next block in the chain.

Programs in the normal mode have no automatic device for recognizing end-of-block; this condition must be handled by programming.

ERROR PROCEDURES

The circuitry of the PTC is designed to detect errors in the communication network and internal parity errors. The machine does not halt. The type and location of errors are made available to the programs, and the service mode is requested. Since this mode has the highest priority, an error program is executed immediately. Programming permits faulty components to be isolated, and enables rapid communication with operating personnel to take place. The programming can include diagnostics to assist in the correction of the malfunctioning component.

In some instances, it may be advisable to have an error routine executed in the normal mode. Otherwise, the machine will remain in the service mode. Since the service mode has the highest priority, the PTC will remain in this mode, thereby preventing other high-priority programs in other modes from being carried out. If the error routine is more urgent than other normal-mode programs, the programmer can arrange his own program priority schedule within the normal mode. This is accomplished as follows: Before the service mode yields control, it saves the contents of the process word containing the instruction counter and operational data registers for the normal mode. In place of this word, the service mode inserts the location of the first instruction in the error routine. Now control is given up by the service mode. When the normal mode gets control, it will commence executing the error program. At the end of this program, the original contents of the normal-mode process word are restored, and the corresponding normal-mode program is carried out.

9 DISK FILE ORGANIZATION

THE 1301 DISK FILE

Most commercial real-time systems require the storage, maintenance, and interrogation of an enormous number of records. Disk
files are usually employed for these purposes. The throughput speed
of a system depends to a large extent on the way data are stored on
the disks, for the organization of the files greatly affects access time to
information.

This chapter discusses various principles and methods for storing
data. Many of these techniques have been used in conventional data
processing systems with disks. They are included here because these
principles are also germane to real-time applications. The chapter also
discusses the record-ready disk feature employed at American Airlines,
and explains how files are organized in this airline reservation system.
It is assumed that the reader has some familiarity with the IBM 1301
disk file.

Information is recorded or retrieved from the 1301 by read-write
heads. A fixed vertical comb containing 40 heads provides one head
for each surface. To access a particular track on a surface, the entire
comb is moved in or out in a horizontal manner, until it is positioned
over the requested track. Thus all 40 heads move together to the
corresponding track on their particular surface when the comb is positioned. Each track has a home address field containing that track's

address, and every record stored on a track is preceded by a gap and a record address field which identifies the record.

Access to a record is obtained by a *seek* command, which positions the comb over the requested track. There is thus a mechanical delay in moving the comb from its present position to the desired track. An additional wait occurs because of the turning of the disks, which rotate completely every 34 milliseconds. The extent of the rotational delay depends on where the requested record happens to be when the read-write head is ready to access the track. The average rotational delay is 17 milliseconds. Transmission rate from disk to core is 70,000 or 90,000 characters per second, depending on the mode of operation.

SEEK TIMES

Since the tracks are arranged exactly over each other, a vertical column of tracks is called a *cylinder*. There are hence 250 cylinders in each module. For mechanical reasons, these cylinders must be conceived as five blocks of 50 cylinders. The time required to move the comb from one block to another is 180 milliseconds. Each block in turn consists of six groups of cylinders; seek time from one group to another within the same block is 120 milliseconds. Within a group, seek time is 50 milliseconds.

One way of estimating the average seek time to a file spread over a large number of cylinders is to proceed as follows:

(1) Choose the cylinder block containing the most cylinders used by the file.
(2) Within this block, ascertain the number of cylinders used in the same group. Multiply this number by 50 milliseconds.
(3) Ascertain the number of remaining used cylinders in this block. Multiply this number by 120 milliseconds.
(4) The number of other cylinders used outside of this block is multiplied by 180 milliseconds.
(5) The sum of these products is divided by the total number of used cylinders.

Here is an example of how average seek time to a file on 100 cylinders might be calculated:

(Number of cylinders in same group)
$$\times \ 50 = 10 \times \ 50 = \ \ \ \ 500 \text{ millisec.}$$
(Remaining cylinders in block) $\times \ 120 = 40 \times 120 = \ \ 4800 \text{ millisec.}$
(Remaining cylinders outside of block)
$$\times \ 180 = 50 \times 180 = \ \ \underline{9000} \text{ millisec.}$$
$$14{,}300 \text{ millisec.}$$

$$\frac{14{,}300}{100} = 143 \text{ milliseconds average seek time.}$$

The average rotational delay of 17 milliseconds gives an average access time of 160 milliseconds.

If a file were dispersed over different modules, seek times could be overlapped, for in this case each set of actuated combs would move independently.

RECORD READY

There are two ways to obtain information from a disk file. In the *cylinder mode*, each track in a designated cylinder is read successively into core by issuing one command from the computer. The other mode consists of accessing one or all of the records on a specified track.

The procedure for obtaining a record from a particular track is to transmit a seek command to the disk. When the seek is completed, an interrupt goes to the computer, which then sends to the disk the commands for reading the requested record. A delay usually ensues while the track turns so as to bring this record under the read-write head. After the interrupt, the channel is unavailable for other transmissions until the record has been read. Hence, the channel is on the average unavailable for one-half the rotational time.

Record ready, a special disk feature for reducing channel usage, is installed at American Airlines.

Eight records are stored on each track of the disk file. On a format track not accessible to the programmer, each of the eight records is preceded by a burst of bits. The number of bits in a burst runs from one to eight. The seek command contains the number of the requested record. With record ready, the interrupt does not occur until there is a burst of bits for the requested record. This burst appears about 2 milliseconds before the record moves under the read-write head. Hence, the channel is available for other purposes until the burst of bits occurs; without this feature, as has been stated, the channel is tied up for an average of one-half the rotational time.

Record ready affects the order of initiation of requests waiting on disk queues in the memory of the main computer. Were this procedure not used, requests would be initiated on a first-in, first-out basis. With record ready, however, a later request may be initiated before an earlier request. This occurs whenever the record requested by the later request is available on its track before the record sought by the earlier request.

INTERCONNECTION OF SYSTEM UNITS

Another special feature which can be installed is a switch enabling disk units or drums to be shared with two 7080's in the same system. This switch is under program control, and enables any disk or drum to be connected at any time to either of the two computers. This device enables both machines to use any of the disk or drum units whenever they are needed, either for engineering diagnostics or for dual processing. Each disk and drum is hence connectable to either 7080 independently of its particular file control unit. Without this *cross-channel switching,* all of the units connected to a computer via a given file control unit can be attached to only one computer at a time.

A similar device enables groups of tapes to be switched from one computer to another.

OBJECTIVES OF FILE ORGANIZATION

It is difficult to generalize upon the characteristics of a good file organization, for the value of any technique depends upon the specific application and its equipment. One definite principle is that the way a file is organized must not dictate the objectives or specifications of a system. The major aims of a method for storing data are as follows:

(1) To provide a means for locating records with a minimum of time and programming effort.
(2) To take advantage of any special characteristics of the equipment, the system, and the data.
(3) To enable the file to be easily loaded, maintained, and controlled.

To access records in minimal time, the addressing technique must be as simple as possible. If extensive calculation is required to compute the location of an item, excessive CPU time may be used. It is important to minimize seek times, for these are a major factor in overall throughput rate.

FACTORS INFLUENCING FILE ORGANIZATION

In storing a file, it is frequently possible to take advantage of certain features of the equipment. For example, the use of the cylinder mode enables about 100,000 characters to be accessed with one movement of the arm comb. Another characteristic of the 1301 which can be utilized is that within groups of cylinders (see above) the maximum seek time is 50 milliseconds. Therefore, it is more efficient to maintain a file within a group than to spread it out. Longer seeks occur in the latter case. Sometimes it is possible to split a file into sections, each of which is stored on a separate module. This technique enables seeks to each section to be overlapped.

The nature of a system often lends itself to some particular form of file organization. For example, if the records in a file are accessed, not randomly, but in a definite sequence, these items can be stored in order in the cylinder mode. If input inquiries enter the machine system in classes, such as by branch office, the file can be arranged so that all branch office records are near neighbors in the file. The movements of the comb in seeking items within branch office are thereby minimized. Another way to reduce seek time is to place records often requested in close succession on neighboring tracks. For example, if programs frequently need *salesman name* soon after they request *part number,* it may be useful to store these items in close juxtaposition.

It may be possible in certain cases to arrange the entry of information from the terminals to make it easier to organize the file. The central computer might poll the terminals in an order which facilitates sequential reference to the disks. Such a system might be possible where each terminal is a branch office. Another possible technique is to sort the queues of disk requests into the same sequence as records stored on the disk units.

Certain characteristics of data can affect file organization. For instance, if descriptive information pertaining to an item is rarely used, it may be better to store the descriptive material elsewhere. This technique can be employed to reduce the size of a frequently accessed file, thereby often reducing total seek time. Sometimes it is well to break up a file on the basis of how frequently the items are requested. For example, if 95% of the input inquiries refer to 10% of the records, it may be desirable to set up a special file or to institute special arrangements to make this 10% of the records the most readily available.

The way in which a file is maintained may suggest a special technique for file organization. Assume, for example, an *accounts receivable* file in which items are stored in the sequence in which they are created. In such a file, records might be stored in invoice number sequence. As days and weeks pass, payments are made, and records are deleted. As a result, the older section of the file tends to become less and less densely packed. Fewer accesses to this part of the file are required in the course of time. On the other hand, the newer section of the file tends to be packed densely, and requires frequent accesses. It may prove useful in such a situation to reload and compress the older part of the file periodically, thereby providing more available space for newer records. The file may be arranged to provide faster access to the newer records, at the expense of the less active older items.

THE EVEN SPREADING OF UNEVENLY DISTRIBUTED CODES

Many problems in file organization stem from the fact that the addresses of machine locations are evenly distributed, whereas code numbers of data are ordered unevenly. The addresses in information storage units are arranged sequentially, but code numbers are often spread out somewhat randomly over a wide range of numbers.

In many applications, data are identified by a control field, or code, such as customer number, salesman number, employee number, and part number. Usually, all of the possible numbers in a control field do not identify items of data. For example, the six-digit code XXXXXX could contain any number from 000000 to 999999, and hence could be used to identify as many as 1,000,000 part numbers. But in practice, this six-digit control field may be utilized merely to identify, say, 20,000 parts. One reason for this apparent wastage of available identification numbers is that it is often necessary to add new items to an inventory. Therefore, empty spaces must be left open for insertions of records. A new product, for instance, may require many new identification numbers.

It is not practical to keep reassigning codes in an actual industrial situation. In fact, control fields usually are assigned so as to classify items. For example, if a six-digit code were used to identify salesmen, the first two digits might be employed to designate state, the next two digits territory, and the last two digits a particular salesman within a territory. A coding system of this type is often desirable for mundane reasons, even though it uses the available identification numbers inefficiently.

It would obviously be wasteful to assign 1,000,000 disk locations to store 20,000 inventory items identified by a six-digit control field. Hence, it is not possible to establish a direct correspondence between code numbers and file-unit addresses. The problem, therefore, is to devise a method for storing the 20,000 items in such a way that control fields can be converted to disk addresses. An optimum technique would generate a unique address for each control field. Statistically speaking, such a method would spread the unevenly distributed control fields evenly over the allotted storage locations.

THE GENERATION OF "SYNONYMS"

The value of a technique for generating addresses depends on how evenly it spreads these addresses over the machine file. If addresses are unevenly distributed, two or more control fields may convert into the same address. Identical addresses created in this way are called "synonyms." Whenever an item is stored, its control field is included. This enables the machine to ascertain the existence of synonyms.

The number of seeks required to access an item in a file is a function of the number and distribution of the synonyms developed by the address-generation technique. The usual way of handling synonyms is to chain the synonym from the first item occupying the file address. If the computer generates an address from a code, but finds an item already in this track location, the machine places a link address in the track. The link address points to another track. The computer now seeks this second track, and stores the item there. If a second synonym occurs, the machine links it with the first synonym, and stores the second synonym in a third track. The general procedure for any number of synonyms is for the computer to trace down the chain, from link to link, finally chaining the presently created synonym to the last synonym in the chain. In retrieving items, the procedure is similar; a chain of synonyms is traced until the requested control number is found.

It is best to locate all synonyms on the same cylinder, if possible. This procedure eliminates the seek time necessary to move the arm comb to another cylinder to access chained synonyms.

As has been stated, the value of a technique for generating addresses depends to a large extent on the number of synonyms produced. Here is an example of a file of 20,000 items, tabulated according to the number of synonyms produced by every item:

Number of synonyms produced	Number of items producing this number of synonyms
0	11,072
1	4175
2	2227
3	1556
4	753
5	146
6	63
7	8
Total	20,000

DIGIT DISTRIBUTION IN THE CONTROL FIELDS

The technique chosen for converting codes into file addresses usually depends upon the distribution of digits in every control field used in the application.

Consider, for example, a five-digit code for a file of 15,000 inventory records. The high-order position of every control field (the leftmost digit) contains one of the digits 0, 1, 2, 3, 4, 5, 6, 7, 8, or 9. A count can be made of how many times each of these 10 digits appears in the high-order position of the code. A similar tabulation can be made for the other four positions in every control field. The following table is thereby formed:

Count of digits in each control field position					
Digit	Position 1	Position 2	Position 3	Position 4	Position 5
0	3800	2100	1400	1200	900
1	700	1000	1900	2000	1100
2	1200	800	1300	4100	800
3	1000	200	1400	800	2000
4	800	2400	1100	2000	300
5	2700	900	1400	700	200
6	1100	2200	1800	3000	4500
7	600	2100	1300	200	2700
8	1300	400	1800	900	500
9	1800	2900	1600	100	2000
Total	15,000	15,000	15,000	15,000	15,000

Since there are 15,000 control fields and 10 possible digits for each position, an even distribution of the digits would consist of 1500 1's, 1500 2's, ... In a perfect spread, the average number of 1's, 2's, etc., in each digit position would be 1500.

The distribution of the digits in the 15,000 record inventory can be analyzed by computing how far each digit count deviates from 1500. In the above example, the high-order position of the control field has 3800 0's, 700 1's, 1200 2's, etc. The deviations (variances) are calculated as follows for position 1 in the control field:

Digit	Count − 1500		Variance
0	3800 − 1500	=	2300
1	700 − 1500	=	800
2	1200 − 1500	=	300
3	1000 − 1500	=	500
.	.	.	.
.	.	.	.
.	.	.	.
.	.	.	.
	Sum of variances =		7600

In computing the sum of the variances, negative signs are ignored, as only the deviation from 1500 is relevant.

Dividing the sum of the variances by 15,000 and multiplying by 100 yields a percentage which shows how far the digit count deviates from a perfect spread. Since the sum of the variances for position 1 is 7600, the measure of spread is

$$\frac{7600}{15,000} \times 100 = 51\%$$

A similar analysis of all of the digit positions results in the following table:

	Digit position				
	1	2	3	4	5
Sum of variances	7600	8400	2200	10,200	10,400
Measure of spread	51	56	15	68	69

The digits 0, 1, . . . , 10 are more evenly distributed in digit position 3 than in the other four positions. The greatest unevenness is in digit position 5.

DIRECT ADDRESSING

The simplest mode of file organization is to arrange for each control field to be the address where its record is stored on the disks. Here the identification code enables each item to be accessed without any further calculations. For this technique to be workable, the control fields must be evenly distributed over the file. In the optimum case, there would be consecutive control fields for every location in the file. Of course, numbering all of the items consecutively requires the storing of 1, 10, or 100 records on each track. This method of storage can only be used when the size of the items is suitable.

EXTRACTING

A simple method for converting control fields to disk addresses is *extraction*. As an example, assume an eight-digit control field composed of a two-digit state field, a two-digit region field, and a salesman-number field of four digits:

SS   RR   NNNN

State   Region   Salesman number

If an analysis of the distribution of digits in each position shows the NNNN digits are well spread, these four digits can be used as a disk address.

If one of the digits in the salesman number field is unevenly distributed, a digit from the state or region field can be used, provided it is evenly distributed. As a general rule, any four well-spread positions in the control field can be used as a file address.

MULTIPLICATION AND DIVISION

Various techniques have been used to generate addresses which spread out evenly.

The multiplication technique squares a control field and extracts the middle digits of the product. If alphabetic characters are present, they are treated as digits. For example, the part number 73A4B6 is regarded as 731426. The square of this number and the middle four digits of this product are:

$$534983993476$$

Address

This technique can be improved by multiplying the four-digit address by the part number. Some of the duplicates which are formed by squaring are in this way eliminated. However, this method requires an extra computational step.

Squaring is not a good approach when the low-order positions are the most evenly distributed. The reason is that in squaring, the low-order positions tend to lose their significance. If the more evenly distributed digits are near the middle of the control field, they have more of an effect on the resulting address.

In the division method, the control field is divided by a constant, and the remainder becomes the disk address. The constant may be either (1) the number of disk locations reserved for the file, or (2) the nearest prime number to the number of disk locations reserved for the file. For example, if the control field is 38429581, and the number of file locations is 10,000, we have either

$$
\begin{array}{r}
3842 \\
10{,}000 \overline{)\,38429581} \\
30000 \\
\hline
84295 \\
80000 \\
\hline
42958 \\
40000 \\
\hline
29581 \\
20000 \\
\hline
9581
\end{array}
$$

(1)

9581 = Disk address

or

$$
\begin{array}{r}
3844 \\
9997 \overline{)\,38429581} \\
29991 \\
\hline
84385 \\
79976 \\
\hline
44098 \\
39988 \\
\hline
41101 \\
39988 \\
\hline
1113
\end{array}
$$

(2)

1113 = Disk address

Some control fields do not adapt well to the division technique because of the distribution in certain digit positions. For example, if the last four digit positions are often identical, many duplicates occur:

$$
\begin{array}{r}
2814 \\
10{,}000 \overline{)\,28145276} \\
20000 \\
\hline
81452 \\
80000 \\
\hline
14527 \\
10000 \\
\hline
45276 \\
40000 \\
\hline
5276
\end{array}
$$

(1)

5276 = Disk address

or

$$
(2) \qquad 10,000 \overline{\smash{\big)}\, 29145276} \quad \begin{array}{r} 2914 \end{array}
$$

$$
\begin{array}{r}
2914 \\
10,000 \overline{\smash{\big)}\, 29145276} \\
\underline{20000} \\
91452 \\
\underline{90000} \\
14527 \\
\underline{10000} \\
45276 \\
\underline{40000} \\
5276 = \text{Disk address}
\end{array}
$$

A COUNT OF DIGITS TECHNIQUE

Code-to-address conversion can be based on a count of digits in each position of the control field. Each count is expressed as a percentage of the 15,000 items in the file. These percentages are cumulated. One-half of the percentages are added to the cumulative totals.

Using position 1 of the control fields tabulated on page 115, this technique yields:

Digit position	Count	Percentage $\left(\dfrac{count}{15,000}\right)$	Cumulative total	Adjusted total (cum. total $+ \frac{1}{2}$ percentage)
0	3800	0.25300	0.00000	0.12700
1	700	0.04700	0.25300	0.27700
2	1200	0.08000	0.30000	0.34000
3	1000	0.06700	0.38000	0.41400
4	800	0.05300	0.44700	0.47400
5	2700	0.18000	0.50000	0.59000
6	1100	0.07300	0.68000	0.71700
7	600	0.04000	0.75300	0.77300
8	1300	0.08700	0.79300	0.83700
9	1800	0.12000	0.88000	0.94000

An *adjusted total* column is calculated for the other positions in the control field in a similar way. These adjusted totals are then used to form a table of constants for every control field from 00000 to 99999:

TABLE OF CONSTANTS

(Constants for positions 2, 3, 4, and 5 have not been calculated.)

Digit	Position in the control field				
	1	2	3	4	5
0	0.12700	xxxxx	xxxxx	xxxxx	xxxxx
1	0.27700	xxxxx	(0.21900)	xxxxx	xxxxx
2	0.34000	xxxxx	xxxxx	xxxxx	(0.48500)
3	0.41400	(0.56100)	xxxxx	xxxxx	xxxxx
4	0.47400	xxxxx	xxxxx	xxxxx	xxxxx
5	0.59000	xxxxx	xxxxx	xxxxx	xxxxx
6	0.71700	xxxxx	xxxxx	xxxxx	xxxxx
7	0.77300	xxxxx	xxxxx	(0.69300)	xxxxx
8	(0.83700)	xxxxx	xxxxx	xxxxx	xxxxx
9	0.94000	xxxxx	xxxxx	xxxxx	xxxxx

Suppose the computer must generate the address of an item whose control field is **83172**. The constant for digit 8 in control position 1 is 0.83700. Assume now that the constants for the other positions in the control field are those circled in the above Table of Constants.

To calculate the address corresponding to item number **83172**, the constants associated with each position in the control field are added together. (Carries from the high-order position are ignored.) We have:

$$
\begin{array}{r}
0.83700 \\
0.56100 \\
0.21900 \\
0.69300 \\
\underline{0.48500} \\
0.79500
\end{array}
$$

This sum is now multiplied by the total number of items in the file (15,000):

$$0.79500 \times 15000 = 11925.00000$$

The digits to the right of the decimal point are dropped. The generated address is **11925**.

RE-EVALUATION OF THE CONVERSION TECHNIQUE

Where an application is such that the character of the file·may change over a period of time, occasional re-examinations of the file-organization techniques may be helpful. For example, the structure of an inventory may undergo an alteration as a result of the deletion, addition, or reassignment of codes. This transformation may affect the evenness of distribution of the addresses generated from the control fields. Hence, it may prove useful to re-evaluate the code-to-address conversion technique from time to time.

PACKING, BLOCKING, AND REPEATING RECORDS

In organizing a file, a decision must be made, in the light of anticipated future expansions and contractions of the file, as to how densely the records should be packed on the disks. It may be useful to allot more disk locations than are needed. This provides room for expansion and in some cases helps to reduce synonyms by spreading out the generated addresses. If 15,000 records were stored in 20,000 suitable locations, the *packing factor* would be 75%.

Another decision must be made concerning the blocking of records on disks. Space is used most economically if each track is entirely occupied by one large record. In this case, no track space is needed for additional record addresses and record gaps. From this standpoint, it would seem desirable to block together as many items as possible into one large record.

Blocking has several disadvantages: To obtain one of the items in a blocked record, the entire record must be read in from the track. Hence, transmission time into memory is longer than it would be for a single item. The channel is also used for a greater period of time. Searching the large record for the particular item which is needed takes a certain amount of CPU time, and more core space must be reserved for the record read in from the disk. Finally, transmission time is longer when a large blocked record is written out. Thus, the saving in disk file storage obtained by blocking must be balanced against the increased throughput time and extra core storage which are thereby required.

In some instances, it may be advantageous to repeat the same record on a track as many times as possible. When a certain record is needed very frequently, this technique reduces access time by decreasing rotational delay.

DIAGONAL STORAGE

The storage of records in diagonal fashion is sometimes of value. An example of this method is shown in Fig. 9-1.

Record 1 is stored in track 001. In track 002, in the same cylinder,

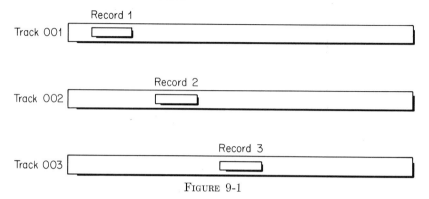

FIGURE 9-1

record 2 is placed in the next record position. Each consecutive record is placed in the next record position on the following track, in a similar way.

When the series of records, 1, 2, 3, . . . are needed, no movement of the arm is required to obtain all of the records, as all of the tracks are in the same cylinder, directly beneath one another. Nor is there any lost rotational time, as the records are so placed on the tracks that the next record is always obtained immediately after its predecessor.

This method is of use only when the information lends itself to this type of storage and retrieval. For example, assume that sales records in the order Jan. 1930, Jan. 1931, Jan. 1932, . . . are stored on the first track. On the next track, arranged diagonally as indicated, are the records for Feb. 1930, Feb. 1931, Feb. 1932, ... If comparative monthly sales figures are needed, a full track is read. Sequential figures are read by utilizing the diagonal mode of storage.

THE DISTRIBUTION TECHNIQUE

The *distribution* method classifies item codes into ranges, as shown on page 123.

The number of file locations assigned to each range is based on the percentage of items falling in the category. For example, 5% of the total disk locations allotted to the file would be made available for items falling into the 000-099 range. In a 1000 record file, 50 locations would be made available for this group of items.

A table in memory contains the upper limit of each range, the first disk address for the category, and the number of disk locations allo-

3 high-order positions of a six-position control field	Number of items in this range
000-099	5%
100-199	5%
200-299	15%
300-399	20%
400-499	10%
500-599	5%
600-699	5%
700-799	10%
800-899	10%
900-999	15%

cated to the records falling within the range. For the above file, this table would take the following form:

Upper limit	First disk address	Number of available locations
099	2000	050
199	2050	050
299	2100	150
399	2250	200
.	.	.
.	.	.
.	.	.

An item whose control field is **173249** belongs in the disk area whose first address is **2050**. The specific address within a range is found by multiplying the last three digits in the control field by the number of available locations for that category, then dividing by the total number of items in the file. Decimal digits are dropped, and the resulting number is added to the first disk address in the file. For example, the address corresponding to **173249** is calculated as follows:

From **173**, we obtain

$$\frac{249 \times 050}{1000} = 12.450$$

$$\begin{array}{r} 2050 \\ \underline{12} \\ 2062 \end{array} = \text{Developed address}$$

FILE INDEXES

One way to organize a disk file is to use an index—a table which contains a disk address for every control field. The index may be kept in core if a small number of records are in the file. If there is a large number of records, the index may be maintained on a disk or drum. A combination of these methods may also be used; part of the index may be kept in core and part on disk.

Here is an example of a file with its index on a disk track: Each record in the file consists of 800 characters. Three records can therefore be kept on each track. If one track per cylinder is used for an index, 39 tracks are available for the storage of records. Hence, 117 records can be placed in each cylinder.

Each control field is constructed to enable the computer to generate the address of the index track in the cylinder where the record is stored. By searching the index track, the computer finds the specific address in the cylinder where the record is located. The total procedure is hence as follows: From a control field, the machine generates the address of an index track. The computer searches the index for the address of the record. Then it accesses the record from the designated location in the cylinder.

Access time can be reduced by storing the index twice in the index track. This technique reduces the rotational delay when the index is being sought. Of course, this method involves extra time when the index is stored on the track. Whenever another record is added to the index, the index must be stored twice.

If more than 117 records produce the same index track addess, this indicates that the cylinder is overloaded. When overloading occurs, the computer arranges for an overflow cylinder, and places the address of this additional cylinder on the index track.

CHAINING TECHNIQUES

Overflow occurs when the control fields in a file convert into more than the allowable number of addresses for a specific track. When the capacity of a track is exceeded, it is necessary to link the generated track address to the address of the overflow track.

One way to chain is to provide a place in the same cylinder for all overflows from tracks in that cylinder. This has the advantage of avoiding additional seek time in repositioning the arm comb; the only delay stems from the rotational time of the chained tracks. But this technique has disadvantages. One problem is that there may be cases where full capacity is never exceeded. Since there are no overflows in such instances, the allotted overflow space is wasted. Another possibility is that in some cylinders more overflows may develop than can be stored in the allotted overflow tracks. Also, care must be taken to prevent the address-conversion technique from converting control fields into the addresses of overflow tracks.

Another approach is not to allot overflow space but to store overflow items in unused space available anywhere in the cylinder. If 1200 records are to be stored on 40 tracks with 30 records per track, it would of course be desirable if exactly 30 control fields converted into each track. In this case, there would be no unused locations and no overflows from any track. However, in practice there are usually tracks with more than 30 synonyms, and tracks with less than 30 synonyms. In a situation of this type, chaining within the same cylinder may be desirable. Here, in Fig. 9-2, is a simple example of this method. Tracks 33, 34, and 35 are shown. The record address contains the control field.

Records 1 and 2 have converted to track 0033, records 3 and 4 have

Track	Address of overflow track	Record address	Record	Record address	Record	Record address	Record
0033	0034	1	- - - -	2	- - - -	7	- - - -

Track	Address of overflow track	Record address	Record	Record address	Record	Record address	Record
0034	0035	3	- - - -	4	- - - -	8	- - - -

Track	Address of overflow track	Record address	Record	Record address	Record	Record address	Record
0035		5	- - - -	6	- - - -	9	- - - -

FIGURE 9-2

converted to track 0034, and records 5 and 6 have converted to track 0035.

Suppose that records 7, 8, and 9 now enter the CPU and are all converted to track 0033. Record 7 is stored in track 0033. Since track 0033 has no vacant positions left, the overflow address is obtained. This points to track 0034, where record 8 is stored. To store record 9, the machine searches through the chain from link to link until an available space is found. Here, the machine, finding no space available in track 0033, goes to track 0034, and from there to track 0035.

Where there are many synonyms, many links in a chain may be traversed before an item is reached. Each of these links is time consuming. This situation may be improved by maintaining an overflow table instead of linked overflow addresses. The overflow table lists each control field and the overflow track where overflow synonyms are stored. This technique uses more positions on the track, but saves time. Of course, there may be an overflow from the overflow table. If this occurs, a second overflow table may be chained to the first overflow table.

LOADING A CHAINED FILE

Where chaining is used, seek times may be reduced by employing a special method for initially loading the disk file. In one technique, all of the records which are to be stored in the track whose address is generated are loaded in a first pass. Overflow items are loaded in a second pass. Prior to loading, the records are ordered by the expected frequency in which they will later be referenced. The most active items are those loaded in the first pass. The least active records are those which are stored as overflows. By following this procedure, access time is reduced, for the chained items requiring the most seeks are the least referenced items in the file.

If records are loaded in one pass without being ordered, overflow items will often come to occupy part of another track whose address will be generated by a record later to be stored. As a result, a chain may be created which could have been avoided by using the two-pass technique.

The following examples illustrate these principles: Assume a file of 15 items, A, B, . . . , O, with room for three records on each track.

Overflow items are placed on the next available track, as shown below. For instance, records *A*, *B*, and *C*, whose control fields are converted to track 1, are stored on track 1. But *D*, which converts to track 1, must be placed on track 2 since track 1 is now full. *E*'s control field generates the address of track 2, where it is stored. *F* converts to track 1 and is placed in track 2. Item *G* also converts to track 1, but by now both track 1 and track 2 are full, so *G* must be stored on track 3.

One-pass loading			
Item	Converted address	Address after loading	Required number of seeks	Chain address after last item in track
A	1	1	1	
B	1	1	1	
C	1	1	1	2
D	1	2	2	
E	2	2	1	
F	1	2	2	3
G	1	3	3	
H	2	3	2	
I	2	3	2	4
J	5	5	1	
K	4	4	1	
L	3	4	2	
M	5	5	1	
N	5	5	1	4
O	5	4	2	
15			23	

$$\frac{23}{15} = 1.53 = \text{average number of seeks}$$

In a simple two-pass loading technique, overflows are not loaded on the first pass; they are placed in vacant locations during the second pass. This eliminates extra chaining. See page 128.

As has been stated, the activity of records in a file has an important effect upon average number of seeks. Continuing with the following two-pass example, assume that items *A*, *G*, and *O* are highly active, accounting for 80% of all of the activity, and that the rest of the file is accessed only 20% of the time. Let *A* be requested 26.7% of the time, *G* 26.7% of the time, and *O* 26.7% of the time. The remaining

				Two-pass loading		
Item	Converted address	After pass 1	After pass 2	Required number of seeks	Chain address
A	1	1		1	
B	1	1		1	
C	1	1		1	3
D	1	not loaded	3	2	
E	2	2		1	
F	1	not loaded	3	2	4
G	1	not loaded	4	3	
H	2	2		1	
I	2	2		1	
J	5	5		1	
K	4	4		1	
L	3	3		1	
M	5	5		1	
N	5	5		1	4
O	5	not loaded	4	2	
15				20	

$$\frac{20}{15} = 1.33 = \text{average number of seeks}$$

20% is divided among the other twelve items. In this case, the average number of seeks is 1.840:

Item	Converted address	After pass 1	After pass 2	Number of seeks	Frequency of use	Number of seeks × frequency of use
A	1	1		1	0.267	0.267
B	1	1		1	0.017	0.017
C	1	1		1	0.017	0.017
D	1	not loaded	3	2	0.017	0.034
E	2	2		1	0.017	0.017
F	1	not loaded	3	2	0.017	0.034
G	1	not loaded	4	3	0.267	0.801
H	2	2		1	0.017	0.017
I	2	2		1	0.017	0.017
J	5	5		1	0.017	0.017
K	4	4		1	0.017	0.017
L	3	3		1	0.017	0.017
M	5	5		1	0.017	0.017
N	5	5		1	0.017	0.017
O	5	not loaded	4	2	0.267	0.534
15					1.005	1.840

Average number of seeks = 1.840
(slight error due to roundoff)

However, if the three most active items, *A*, *G*, and *O* are loaded first, they do not become overflow items. As demonstrated below, this technique reduces average seek time substantially:

Item	Converted address	After pass 1	After pass 2	Number of seeks	Frequency of use	Number of seeks × frequency of use
A	1	1		1	0.267	0.267
G	1	1		1	0.267	0.267
O	5	5		1	0.267	0.267
B	1	1		1	0.017	0.017
C	1	not loaded	3	2	0.017	0.034
D	1	not loaded	3	2	0.017	0.034
E	2	2		1	0.017	0.017
F	1	not loaded	4	3	0.017	0.051
H	2	2		1	0.017	0.017
I	2	2		1	0.017	0.017
J	5	5		1	0.017	0.017
K	4	4		1	0.017	0.017
L	3	3		1	0.017	0.017
M	5	5		1	0.017	0.017
N	5	not loaded	4	2	0.017	0.034
15				20		1.090

Average number of seeks = 1.090
(slight error due to roundoff)

ANOTHER INDEXING METHOD

Another technique is based on the storing of the records in sequential order, starting with track 001 of the first cylinder. A *track table* constructed for each cylinder contains the last control field placed on each track. Hence, for each track number from 001 to 039, the table contains the highest control field stored in that track. When an entire cylinder has been filled, its track table is stored in its track 000. The next records in sequence are placed in the following cylinder, and a track table is formed for that cylinder. This process is continued until all of the records are stored. As each cylinder is completed, a *cylinder table* is formed in core, consisting of the number of the cylinder and the highest control field stored in that cylinder.

Records are retrieved as follows: A lookup in the cylinder table locates the cylinder where the record is stored. A seek to this cylinder obtains the track table. A lookup in the track table locates the track on which the record is stored. A final seek, involving no head movement, obtains the actual record.

ADDITIONS TO THE FILE

Where it is necessary to make frequent additions to a file, it may be useful to maintain an index of overflow items.

When a new record appears, the machine generates its track address. If there is an empty location in this track, this space is used for the new item. If the track is full, the computer ascertains whether one or more of these stored records are overflows from another track. (Checking for an overflow is carried out by converting a record's control field to a track address, and comparing the generated track address with the address of the track where the record is stored.) If an overflow record is found, it is replaced by the new item, which belongs on that track. The dispossessed overflow record is relocated to another track by an available-space subroutine which also changes the overflow address of that item in the overflow table. When a track is completely filled with nonoverflow records, a new item for that track is treated as a regular overflow.

If a record is to be deleted from a file, and that item is an overflow record, the item must be blanked out on the track, and its control field and address must be removed from the overflow table. If the record is not an overflow item, it is merely blanked out on the track. By the way, to delete an item, it is not necessary to blank out the record on the track. It suffices merely to blank out the record address on the track to prevent an equal comparison whenever a seek occurs for the item.

FILE ORGANIZATION IN SABRE

In an airline reservation system, the organization of disk storage is volatile. Usage of the disks is continually changing in a random manner, and it is not possible to predict in advance what areas will be employed at any given moment in the future.

An airline's product is a perishable inventory consisting of tens of thousands of seats on flights leaving every day. In most instances, customers call the airline in advance to make reservations for a flight. As has been stated, whenever a reservation is made, a PNR (passenger name record) is prepared by the machine. This record is based on information entered into the terminal set by the agent. Numerous references to the PNRs are necessary after a reservation is made. For example, the airline accesses the PNRs to make up flight manifests (lists of passengers), to process wait lists of customers, and to enter flight schedule changes. Passenger name records must be altered when passengers change their itineraries or enter new information.

Since reservations may be made a year in advance, a large, random number of PNRs must be kept available for immediate access. The need for dynamic disk allocation arises from the fact that the number of stored passenger records for flights during the next year is continually in flux. It is not possible to preassign areas in the disks to passenger name records. Hence, a pool of available disk storage is maintained. Fixed location directories keep track of the allocation of space. Bit positions in the directories indicate whether or not each area in the pool is assigned for use as a PNR.

The computer obtains the address of a requested PNR through a lookup in a *gross index,* followed by a lookup in a *fine index.* The gross index is ordered by days. Within each day is listed all of the flights leaving during that period of time. Each flight-date points to its particular fine index. A fine index consists basically of a list of passengers who have made reservations for a given flight-date. For lookup convenience, this list usually consists of five alphabetic groupings, each of which has its own address. Along with the name of each passenger in the fine index is the address of that passenger's PNR. Hence, to access a PNR, the machine ascertains the day of departure, the flight number, and the name of the passenger. The computer uses the date to go to the proper gross index. The flight number in this gross index points to the fine index for that flight-date. If this fine index is broken up into alphabetic groupings, the computer goes to the grouping containing the passenger's last name. Upon finding the passenger's name in the fine index, the machine obtains the address of his PNR.

The address of the gross index for a particular flight on a given date is computed from its date and its flight number. Each flight-date record in the gross index consists of seven words. The first five words are reserved for the addresses of the five alphabetic groupings in the fine index. The sixth word contains the address of a passenger wait list. If there are no passengers waiting to get reservations in the event of cancellations, this word consists of zeros. The seventh word contains the address of an extra section of the flight; it is zero if no extra section is scheduled.

Since flight schedules are known in advance, the gross index can be maintained in fixed file locations. However, the size of each fine index is a function of the number of passengers who have made reservations for that flight-date. Therefore, file space must be allotted to the fine index at random, just as space is allocated randomly for PNR storage.

The fine index uses blocks, each containing as many as 17 four-word entries. The first two words of each entry consist of 12 characters into which are compressed a passenger name and associated information. The other two words contain the address of the PNR and various control fields.

The gross index for the next 4 days' flights is maintained on the drums, to provide more rapid access to this information. The gross index for the remaining 361 days is kept on the disks. At the end of each day, the fifth day's gross index is moved from disk to drum, and becomes the new fourth day's gross index.

INVENTORY OF SEATS

The basis of the entire Sabre system is the inventory of seats on future flights. Whenever a customer makes a reservation, the inventory must be updated by the number of seats reserved for the chosen flight. The flights departing in the near future tend to receive the most inquiries from customers. To provide rapid access to these records, the inventories for a certain number of days in the future (usually from 15-30) are maintained on the drums. The exact number of days' inventories kept on the drums is adjustable, as this number depends upon the amount of drum storage available. Flight inventories for the remainder of the year are kept on disk.

Two gross indexes to flights are maintained on the drums. Each gross index consists of 1000 consecutive words, every location referring to a flight number from 000-999. Each of these words contains the address of a fine index. A fine index is composed of one-word records, each pointing to an inventory record for a flight on a certain date.

Fine indexes are kept only for flights for which one or more seats have been reserved. If no seat has been reserved for a flight-date, the word in the fine index contains the address of an *image record* from which an inventory record can be created. If no flight is scheduled for a date, the word contains a special code.

One of the gross indexes is maintained for the inventory records for the current 30 days. The fine index for these records is stored on the drum. The address of the drum fine index is also computable from flight information sent in by agents from the terminals. The other gross index refers to flights for the next 335 days; its fine index is kept on the disks.

Inventory records are constructed when the first reservation for a flight-date is made. All inventory records when created are stored on disk; if they belong on the drum, they are brought over by a nightly file-maintenance program. The program which creates the inventory records uses the record-hold feature (see below, page 159) provided by the control program. This holds the appropriate fine index record, thereby preventing two agent messages from simultaneously creating the same inventory record.

The nightly file-maintenance program includes a cycling procedure. This action transfers one future day's inventory records from disk to drum; the corresponding gross and fine indexes are correspondingly adjusted. While file maintenance is occurring, there may of course be interrogations of the inventory records by agents. Since, at this moment, only part of the cycling may have been completed, provision is made to enable the control program to know where the affected records are at this stage of the file-maintenance procedure.

Why are not the gross index and fine index combined into one index? Although 1000 locations are used for the gross index, not all of these locations represent scheduled flights. Where a location does not correspond to a flight number, the location is filled with zeros; since the location is never used, it does not refer to a block of days in the fine index. However, if the gross index and fine index were combined, these slots would have to be maintained for nonexistent flights, thereby wasting considerable drum storage.

Access to the inventory records is needed by the Sabre programs for a variety of purposes. However, a large number of the requests from agents merely require availability information, and do not involve updating the inventory or making use of flight description data. The customer often wants to know simply whether from one to four seats are available on a given flight-date. To obtain this information from the inventory (assuming the date is within the days maintained on the drums) requires three accesses to the drum (including one access to the gross index and one access to the fine index).

To reduce the time required for mere availability information, a special availability file is maintained. As with inventory, a certain number of days' records are kept on the drums, and the remainder on the disks. This file, stored in fixed locations, is arranged as follows: Each day is allotted four drum records. Each record contains 64 words. The first record for a day indicates one-seat availability for the flights scheduled for that day. The second record indicates two-seat availability. The third and fourth records indicate three-seat and four-seat availability. Within each record, 55 words, or 1980 bits, can be used as availability indicators; and eight words, or 288 bits, can be used to indicate whether extra sections are scheduled for that flight-date. Each bit position corresponds to a leg of a flight. (If a flight is not nonstop, there will be arrivals and departures at intervening points, called *legs*.)

Thirty consecutive blocks of 64 words each are also maintained in core to indicate the availability of from one to five seats on flight-dates of other airlines. Each of these 30 blocks corresponds to a day's flights.

FILE DEGRADATION

One of the problems in real-time systems is that of maintaining efficiency during periods when file units are inoperative. The system as a whole must be able to continue operating without serious impairment and at an optimal level under conditions of equipment degradation. As a case in point, let us consider the Sabre procedures when one or more of the drums becomes temporarily unusable.

There are six drums in the Sabre system, in addition to the disks. The drums are used as a rapid-access bulk-storage medium for high-activity items such as programs and inventory records.

All information on the drums is maintained in duplicate form on the disks. Hence, if one or more drums become temporarily inoperative, it is possible to rely upon the duplicate records on the disks. If the control program found that requested data was stored on a drum currently being repaired, its procedure could be to obtain this information from the appropriate disk. However, this mode of operation would not provide maximum efficiency, for the disk accesses to the needed items would take much longer than the usual drum references.

Therefore, as soon as a drum is disconnected temporarily from the system, the control program reorganizes the contents of the remaining five drums. Utilizing the disk duplicates of the malfunctioning drum, the control program stores the most frequently needed information from the entire six drums on the remaining five drums. The least active data is no longer kept on drums at all, for in reorganizing the contents of the remaining drums, the control program replaces less important information with often-needed records from the inoperative drums. If two drums were undergoing repair, the most active records on these drums would be placed somewhere on the other four drums, replacing the less frequently needed information on these four drums. The control program would utilize the disk duplicate records of the two drums under repair when it reorganized the contents of the remaining four drums.

Another approach presently being contemplated in a system with four drums is to use three of these units for high-activity records, and to employ the fourth as a fallback drum.

One difficulty in fallback procedures is the necessity of reduplicating the duplicated data contained on a unit which is temporarily out of service. This duplicated information must be reduplicated to provide protection in the event of a second failure. At one installation, if a 1301 becomes inoperative, the duplicates it contains are reduplicated on a fallback 1301 reserved for this purpose. One problem involved in this reduplication is that it takes from 4-5 minutes. During this time, the real-time system cannot operate. Is it advisable not to reduplicate, thereby risking the possibility of another disk failure (in which case the information would be lost), or is it better to spend these minutes in reduplication, even at peak periods?

The techniques chosen for storing information on disk files must be considered from the standpoint of the fallback procedures, for certain modes of file organizations may cause the fallback method to become unduly complicated and time consuming.

10 PLANNING AND MANAGING A REAL-TIME SYSTEM

SYSTEMS STUDIES

Numerous problems in the planning and implementation of conventional data processing systems are intensified by the greater complexity of real-time installations.

In setting up any computing system, the first step is to understand its information-handling requirements. In commercial applications, this requires extensive communication between the planners of the electronic data processing system and the methods or accounting personnel in the business. In a large system, defining the specifications is usually a tortuous process which occupies a team of systems analysts for many man-years, even if the procedures are written up. Often large parts of the system consist of traditional practices handed down over the years from one person to another, and innumerable interviews are necessary to elicit the complete details. The duties of each clerical person interconnect with those of others, and sometimes no one individual has a good overall comprehension of the entire procedures. It is very difficult to keep in mind how all of the segments of the system interlink. Where writeups exist, they may be out-of-date, and hence may not incorporate later changes. Statements of the procedures may be unclear or unintentionally misleading.

The methods and procedures of a business often evolve rather than being planned. As needs arise, systems groups devise special methods or modify old procedures. New departments may require different reports. Products may be dropped, plants built, offices opened, management centralized or decentralized, and company structure reorganized. Along with these changes occur shifts and reassignments of personnel and management. The processing of information reflects such happenings. Master files are added or become obsolete, code numbers are expanded or restructured, exceptions are introduced or grafted on to existing methods, and new regulations are incorporated into the procedures. Sometimes a business system resembles an organism which has arisen through a long evolutionary process. Vestigial organs may remain in the form of inconsistencies, unnecessary methods, or inefficiencies. Because of its complexity, a large system is expensive to revise or overhaul. For this reason, it often continues to evolve and adapt through the years.

There is no definite point where procedural analysis is complete and machine system design begins. Typically there is an iterative relation between the two phases. After a certain amount of study, the planners of the electronic data processing system begin to feel that they have sufficient understanding to start laying out the broad outlines of the computing installation. In the course of planning, further questions arise about the specifications, so they return to learn more about the procedures. This additional information may often affect the design of the system. After a number of iterations, the planners conclude that overall design is now more or less complete. Now the problem is parceled out among several groups of programmers.

As each group delves into the specific details of data layouts and flowcharting, it tends to raise numerous additional questions, necessitating further inquiries into system requirements. In answering these questions, unexpected problems often arise. It may turn out that an entire aspect of the specifications has never been adequately studied or understood. For example, under special circumstances certain item codes may require special handling, or at certain times of the year summaries may have to be produced in a different sequence. Any of a large number of facts previously not properly understood may unexpectedly emerge as important specifications. As a result, it may be necessary to make a complete overhaul of the planning.

Another factor which may cause upheavals is the realization that it is necessary or desirable to modify certain practices upon converting the present system to a computer. Very often the speed and versatility of a machine system, particularly one which is real-time, make possible improvements in existing procedures. These changes may greatly modify the planning of the data processing system. The possibility of such alterations is particularly great when there are no previously existing procedures. This may occur not only in commercial situations, but in scientific, military, and engineering applications as well, wherever completely new plants or equipment have been constructed. In such cases, it is necessary to start from the beginning in exploring the specifications. Under these circumstances, inevitable changes in the requirements will frequently necessitate large-scale revisions in the planning.

THE PROBLEMS OF PROGRAMMERS

Revisions or assignments of new programs also may occur because of changes in planning and in response to improved awareness of procedural requirements. The result of this evolution is the preparation of numerous interrelated programs by a large staff of programmers. Since the output of any one program may be the input for many other programs, complete standardization of input and output formats among interconnected programs is necessary. Rigid documentation becomes indispensable. Each programmer must keep all other related programmers informed, not only about changes he makes in his input or output formats, but also about revisions in his program's procedures. Communication of modified specifications is vital. Each programmer tends to be deluged with memos which may or may not be relevant to his programs. Ultimately, several thick loose-leaf notebooks are needed to hold all of the specifications and specification revisions. There is also the problem of where to file each modification when it arrives. Changes in specifications take the form of addenda or errata sheets. Sometimes there are addenda to addenda, followed by errata sheets and more addenda.

Even after a programmer has faithfully read and filed new specifications or revisions, he must incorporate these concepts, procedural changes, and data specifications into his programs. It is a matter of common observation that programmers tend to forget many of the details in their programs a short while after they have been written. Detailed recall of a completed program may last only for several weeks, particularly if the person has already become busy with other programs. Even when he returns to his coding sheet on Monday morning, a programmer may need 5 or 10 minutes to reimmerse himself in the details he was working on last Friday night. Furthermore, it is somewhat frustrating to delve into flowcharts and coding, to adjust a program to new or changed specifications. It is still more frustrating when such adjustments are needed frequently. Many errors in logic and coding arise when changes are incorporated into existing programs. A formidable problem exists when the author of a program is no longer present. Programmers, like everyone else, occasionally shift jobs, resign, get married, die, and have babies. The revision of someone else's program is very difficult, and often results in logical or coding errors.

The most trivial of changes in requirements or formats may cause grief and hardship to another programmer. For example, a bit which must be appended to a field may force a programmer to revise completely a work area. This may necessitate altering the addresses which refer to the various fields in the work area. In turn, these changes may affect other parts of the coding.

Special organization structures may be useful in achieving standardization of input and output formats. Some specifications may be more convenient for certain programmers than for others. Other standards may greatly inconvenience some programmers. Several organizational techniques are possible for handling these problems. Group meetings are democratic, but tend to be time consuming and lead to futile argumentation. Decisions may be made by a manager after consultation with the affected people. Or a special board may have authority for making decisions. Isolated truces among individual programmers should not be permitted, for these agreements may unwittingly affect other programmers. A further function of a mediation board may be to enforce proper documentation of all changes to the system.

Breaking programs up into subroutines helps to avoid many problems. Designed to accomplish specific tasks, each subroutine constitutes an independent unit which in combination with other such units can execute very complex procedures. Subroutinization may hence reduce the programming effort. This technique also facilitates the incorporation of new specifications into the system. It is easier to change several subroutines than to dig into a long program to make revisions. Debugging many short routines is easier than testing a number of long programs.

In the Mercury system, difficulties resulting from changed input and output formats were lessened as follows: Each operational program was preceded and followed by short sequences of instructions called the *prefix* and *suffix*. One of the main functions of a prefix is to store inputs to its operational program in locations where they will be addressed by the program. The suffix places the output into a format used by a successor program. Responsibility for communication of inputs and outputs among programs is thus assigned to prefixes and suffixes. These subroutines also communicate between operational programs and the control program. Alterations in input or output formats are reflected mainly in prefixes and suffixes, rather than in the programs themselves.

When first planning layouts, it is advisable to leave ample room in records for unanticipated fields which may be needed by other programs as the system gradually takes shape. If area for expansion is not left available, a good deal of labor may later have to be expended in revising both these records and the instructions which refer to them.

It is desirable to separate the control program as much as possible from the operational programs, so that the individuals writing operational programs need not concern themselves with the special problems of real-time systems. The task of the operational programmer is easier if he can confine most of his attention to his own problems, rather than also concerning himself with general control functions.† For this reason, as we have seen, various macros are made available to the operational programmer for carrying out procedures such as *find, file,* and *rent.*

One important responsibility of management in a real-time system is to break procedures down properly for assignment to programmers. The manner in which this is done affects both linkage time during execution and the interaction of programs during testing.

SYSTEMS STANDARDS

Inconsistencies in specifications which appear when one program calls upon another program may cause mistakes which are not easy to locate under the difficult conditions of real-time testing. At one large real-time installation, a detailed standards manual was prepared to alleviate such conditions. Writeups of program specifications, for example, must conform rigidly to the following structure:

† However, from a testing standpoint, it is very desirable for operational programmers to understand the control program.

1. *Purpose of program:* A statement, in less than three paragraphs, of what the program does and why it is needed. This declaration must be in sufficient detail to convey the basic function of the program without requiring the reader to peruse the specification further.

2. *Restrictions on the program:* A statement of constraints on the use of the program. Among the possible sources of these restrictions are the control program, the time of day, and features of other operational programs. Here are two examples: (1) "This program can be entered only by the time-initiated supervisor at 2 A.M.," (2) "The inventory file-maintenance tapes must be on line."

3. *Size of program:* A statement of how much core is needed for the instructions and constants constituting the program. The number of blocks of core storage is also specified.

4. *Inputs to program:* A detailed description of every record, field, character, or bit needed as input to the program, and where each is located. If some or all of these inputs are described in a data-specification writeup, it is sufficient to list the fields, stating the name of the data specification.

A statement of all positions in the entry block used for the input message (input message area). In addition, all positions used in the entry block for temporary storage and intercommunication among operational programs (operational storage area) must be specified. A listing of all request word areas must be included.

5. *Outputs from program:* A statement of all intermediate data written out at any time by the program. This includes records such as those stored in files or sent to agents as messages. All records, fields, characters, and bits changed must be described.

A listing of all records, fields, characters, or bits which are final outputs. If these are referred to in data specifications, each such data specification is listed. Outputs which occur under all possible conditions must be specified. The final states of the request word areas, the input message area, and the operational storage area must be described in detail.

6. *Cross references:* The name and code number of all data specifications to which references are made, indicating whether this data is created or modified by the program. A statement of the average number of file accesses required. A list of the macros used by the program.

7. *Linkage:* A statement of all other programs which this program enters, and how control is returned. The name and code number of each linked program is included, along with the number of times each such program is used.

8. *Method:* A written explanation and a flowchart of the program. This information is of value, not simply for present coding and testing, but for future understanding of the system.

PROGRAM DOCUMENTATION †

Whenever a person is assigned a program, he establishes a special notebook or binder for information concerning this program. This information must appear in the following exact sequence:

(1) Title index from the assembly program (titles are the headings preceding instruction groups).
(2) List of instructions from the assembly program.
(3) Constants and areas after assembly.
(4) Symbolic analyzer assembly (cross index of where various data and constants are referred to in the program). This is useful when changes must be introduced into the program.
(5) Memory print of the program block.
(6) Patches (inserts) listings. It is often not economical to reassemble a program when an alteration is necessary. This is particularly the case when errors are found in debugging, or when system requirements are changed.
(7) Detailed flowchart, cross-referenced against the coding by page and line number.
(8) Program specification.
(9) Data specifications.

The programmer keeps this notebook in his own file while he is preparing the program, along with his card decks. After completing the first phase of testing (see page 153), the notebook is placed in a central file maintained for all programs. The assembled deck and the source-language deck are also placed in special files. Persons desiring to use any of this material must obtain approval to do so, and must sign out the material they withdraw.

† Program documentation is, of course, only one part of the documentation required for the entire system.

COORDINATION FUNCTIONS

A special board, called the *systems evaluation and control group* (SEC), reviews current activities, and monitors all specifications, writeups, and requests for changes. Each member of the SEC tends to develop special familiarity with some area of the system, and every individual on the board, particularly the group leader, acquires an overall grasp of the application. The SEC enforces adherence to standards. By reviewing all specifications and specification changes, it seeks to spot incompatible methods and logical errors. The general function of the systems evaluation and control group is to provide communication and coordination among all activities.

One person on the project, assigned as librarian, maintains a file of all finished material, and keeps a log of work in progress. Whenever a group leader allots a task, he prepares a *status log sheet,* and gives the task a code number. The log sheet, kept by the librarian, lists the person or group working on each program or procedure. Upon the successful termination of each phase of an assignment, the librarian enters the completion date in the log sheet, along with the approval of the group leader. Indications on the log sheet state whether a program is under revision and when revision is complete.

The librarian's log book enables the directors of the project to know the exact status of all specifications and programs at any time. Without a logging procedure, it is difficult to ascertain how the project is developing—what programs are complete, under test, or being coded, and what specifications are under preparation. By indicating that a given program is under revision, the log book prevents other programmers from making the error of using a routine now being altered.

The librarian follows strict procedures in making entries into the log book. The programmer or specification writer must turn in his completed material to the librarian, who enters the completion date in the log. The librarian forwards completed material to the appropriate people for their approval. Upon approval, the librarian enters the date of approval in the log. Similar procedures are followed for requests for changes in specifications or programs.

Rapid reference to the logging system is provided by a punched-card procedure. Each page in the log book is keypunched, and the cards are periodically listed. The listing contains the following information:

(1) All program specifications with their current status, such as original, revised, reissued, coded, tested. Dates are included.

(2) All data specifications with their current status and dates.

(3) Names of all people who have prepared specifications.

(4) Program and data specification cross references. These include:

    (a) Programs which enter other programs. These cross references indicate all of the programs which have acted upon an entry during its life. Hence, they facilitate tracing possible sources of an error. When program changes are necessary, the cross references enable other affected programmers to be notified.

    (b) Data specifications used in each program specification.

    (c) Data specifications used in creating another data specification.

CHANGES IN SPECIFICATIONS

Whenever a member of the staff believes that a change in the system is necessary or desirable, he must follow a fixed procedure. First he discusses the problem with his group leader. If the group leader approves the change, the individual prepares a formal written request in triplicate. On this request, he states his suggestions, his reasons, and the alternate possibilities.

The proposal is now submitted to the SEC, which reviews the request, assigns it a number, and forwards it to the appropriate group leaders. In responding to the proposal, the group leaders indicate whether or not the proposal is acceptable and why. All involved project members place their signatures on the document after they make their decision.

PROGRAMMING RESTRICTIONS

Some restrictions on operational programs in real-time applications pertain mainly to clerical aspects of programming. For example, in one large system, the standards manual requires all programmers to use unique 10-character tags with all data fields. In the absence of this procedure, two or more programs might employ the same labels for data, and the assembly program could not assemble them both at the same time. Another advantage of tag conventions is that these rules make it easier for an outsider to understand each program and to refer to the data specifications.

The basic tag consists of four numeric characters, consisting of the code number of the data specification. This is followed by from one to five letters chosen by the person who prepares the data specification. The 10th character designates the request word area for which the record is destined. Use of this character prevents the field from being assigned to different request word areas.

All instruction tags must begin with the program specification number and the program segment number. The first instruction of each segment must have START after the program specification and program segment number. For example, the first instruction of the first segment of program specification 200A would appear as 200A1START. The first instruction of the second segment of program specification 200A would appear as 200A2START.

Certain constants used frequently remain permanently in core. The list of these constants is increased or revised as necessary. Over a period of time, the SEC group may include new constants which are actively accessed. Among the constants kept permanently in core are the digits zero through nine, with plus and minus signs and with no signs. Numerous special characters are kept permanently in core, as are various special bit configurations.

Other constraints on programmers result from the specific features of the equipment utilized. For example, the 7080 moves information from one part of its memory to another by means of an instruction which relies upon a *record mark* to terminate transmission of characters. A record mark is a special 7080 character. Therefore, if a programmer places a record mark anywhere within his program or data, the control program will only transmit the information prior to the special character, and the remaining characters will not be moved. Hence, the standards manual restricts the use of record marks.

Another unique aspect of the 7080 is its 15 variable-length auxiliary storage units (ASUs). These registers function somewhat as extra accumulators. In a real-time system, they must be assigned a fixed length, to avoid confusion. Since these lengths may be altered by instructions, the programmers must be constrained from changing the assigned size of the ASUs. Certain ASUs used by the control program are not available to the operational programmers.

Various characteristics of real-time systems necessitate imposing restrictions on the programmers. For example, programs must not refer to core storage outside of the program itself and its working storage area. Since operational programs cannot handle any input-output functions, programmers are forbidden to use *control* or *select* instructions. Programmers must become sufficiently familiar with the control program to be able to use the input-output macros properly. Programmers are also restricted from using halt instructions (otherwise the main processor could come to a stop).

MAN-MACHINE COMMUNICATION

It is necessary to place some constraints on the operators of the terminal sets. For example, if an agent is not required to type information into the system in a definite format, the machine must utilize subroutines to find out where fields are located in the incoming messages. Each call upon a subroutine involves activity of the control program and linkage among programs. Where a large volume of messages enter a system, the proliferation of such subroutines may adversely affect throughput time.

A similar problem occurs if the operators at the terminals are permitted to make many unusual responses to procedural situations. In each case, the computer must be prepared to recognize and handle the information sent in by the agent. One aspect of planning a real-time system is the training of the humans who will communicate with the machine. At American Airlines, a conversational interaction exists between the central computer and the agents at the terminals. Agents must learn how to enter various inquiries and information, and how to react to machine messages typed out under various conditions. A terminal set attached to a small computer simulated this man-machine interaction for training purposes.

Simulation was also used in Project Mercury for training humans at the control centers. The computer would flash simulated displays at these control centers, depicting various conditions such as the need for abort or re-entry. The human operators learned how to interpret these displays so as to initiate the proper actions under real-time conditions.

Restrictions may also be related to the nature of the communication equipment. The length of an output message, for example, must not be longer than the size of the remote buffer in certain installations.

PERIPHERAL UNITS

All records destined for storage on the disk files must start with an identification field in the first three characters of the record. The first two characters designate the type of record, and the third the type of block. The programmer inserts this identification when he creates the record. The three characters perform these functions:

(1) Enables verification that a record read from file is the requested type of record.
(2) Enables verification that a record written on file has been correctly written.
(3) Provides a simple way of determining the size of a block.
(4) Provides a simple way of determining whether the record is chained, and if so, its location in the chain.

The identification is also used by the file-maintenance program, which searches the file for records no longer in use.

PROGRAM MODIFICATION

Certain programs have a heavy usage. For example, programs which convert dates from different time zones to a standard date, and programs which compute file addresses are in frequent demand. Such programs remain permanently in core. If such a program is modified, it is permanently changed unless it is initialized. To insure uniformity, the established standard requires all such programs to be initialized at the beginning of the program.

In one 7080 installation, all programs not permanently assigned to core are kept in file storage, or in upper memory. Hence, if any such program is modified, such modifications are lost when the program yields control through a departure macro. This is because a program in the working storage area is destroyed after it gives a departure macro. When an entry regains control, the control program provides it with an original copy of the program. Hence, dynamic program modification must be planned so that the modification need not be retained over the period between the yielding and regaining of control. Recommended practice is to avoid modification of operational programs by using methods such as setting switches in the operational storage area.

POST-PROCESSING OF ASSEMBLED PROGRAMS

At American Airlines all assembled operational programs pass through a post-processor, which performs a number of functions. A common pool of constants is formed by extracting the constants from each individual program. In this way, duplication of constants is avoided. The post-processor conserves program storage space on the drums by packing small program segments together in the standard blocks. Another task of the post-processor is to establish linkages between segments for transfers of control between segments.

SEGMENTATION OF PROGRAMS

The way in which an operational program is broken up into segments may seriously increase the throughput time of a system. It is undesirable to create a situation where numerous transfers between segments are necessary. Each time another segment is called upon, a time-consuming linkage through the control program occurs. If the other segment must be read into core from the disks, another long period of time is consumed. Perhaps the worst practice is to break a program loop into two segments.

11 THE TESTING OF PROGRAMS IN REAL-TIME SYSTEMS

SYSTEM TESTING

In both the American Airlines and Mercury projects, many of the greatest problems arose in the testing of programs. These experiences led to the development of special techniques for program testing in real-time systems.†

A basic rule in real-time testing is to design the system from the beginning so as to include all of the testing facilities which will be necessary. Planning which neglects the problems of testing can lead to difficulties when the system is readied for use. Of major magnitude is the preparation of program testing facilities. This project requires many man-years of programming, and must be scheduled so that the testing aids are available when needed. In one large real-time installation, more than twice as much labor was expended in preparing utility programs and programs for testing and simulating the system than was used in writing the operational programs.

In conventional batch-processing, programs are tested by executing small parts of a program in sequence. If a programmer seeks to test too large a portion of his program at once, he usually finds that the situation has become too complex for him to handle.

---

† As stated in the Acknowledgments, much of the material in this chapter is drawn from a special report. This report was oriented towards the needs of a particular installation. Hence, in some instances certain techniques are not equally necessary for all real-time systems, but are unique to this installation.

The same principle exists in the testing of real-time programs. Indeed, it is even more important in this case, for in real-time systems each program does not retain control during its entire execution, and two or more entry blocks may use the same program at the same time. For these reasons, tracing and uncovering errors may become extremely difficult and laborious. Another complication in real-time applications may be the presence of more than one processing unit.

Each segment of an operational program must obviously be debugged before any further testing can occur. Next, all of the segments of a program must be tested together. Where a group of programs (a *package*) performs some particular function, the entire package is tested after each of the individual programs has been debugged. This step is followed by the testing of all *threads*. A thread consists of all of the programs or packages needed to process an entry. Finally each thread must be tested with two or more entries. Where there is more than one processing unit in the system, each subsystem must be separately tested, then tested together with the other processing units.

It is desirable to use test data prepared both by the programmer and by other individuals. Test data designed by the programmer himself usually uncovers obvious errors. However, where a program has many possible combinations of paths, the programmer's own data may not call out all possibilities. Hence, it is advisable to arrange for another source of test data. These data may either be specifically designed for testing purposes by other persons, or may be actual data obtained from current field operations. Another source of test data is desk set operators who are being trained.

To achieve speed and accuracy during the early testing phases, transactions enter the system from tape. The rate of input from a person typing at a terminal is slow, and typists tend to make errors. On the other hand, entries on tape can be checked in advance for accuracy.

In the Mercury system, tapes containing simulated inputs were also used for testing programs and for ascertaining if the system would function properly under various loads. Artificial data were prepared by computing a flight path from certain initial conditions. Given this orbit, it was possible to compute what inputs would be received from the radar sites at various times. A tape was then prepared which contained these inputs. Noise and error were deliberately included along with the data on this tape. Testing with tape required writing a simulation input control program (SIC). The running system was interrupted every 5 milliseconds by a clock. This trap gave control to SIC, which read the simulated input tape and placed the appropriate data into the memory buffer areas. SIC also simulated the interrupts which would have occurred had the data been entered in real-time over the data communication channel.

A testing procedure for a large real-time system might consist of the following seven phases:

PHASE I

This phase utilizes a simulated control program which imitates all of the functions the actual control program performs in an operational situation. No disk files are used, and only one program runs at a time (there is no multiprogramming). Input and output are by means of tape.

There are three parts to phase I:

(a) The testing of individual program segments.
(b) The testing of threads, one at a time.
(c) The tracing of different paths through each thread, by using different entries.

One reason why phase I uses a simulated control program is that there is not enough space in core for debugging aids when the actual control program is in operation. Testing aids, such as tracers and memory prints, occupy thousands of core positions. Most of these positions are needed by the control program when it is in use.

Another reason for employing simulation in phase I is that the complete machine system may not have been delivered when testing begins. It is less expensive to start testing before installation of all of the machine units.

In addition, many of the operational programs may be ready for testing before the control program is complete. Simulation of the control program therefore hastens the debugging of these operational programs. Furthermore, since the control program retains undiscovered errors for a period of time, it is easier to test operational programs in an error-free environment. If there are possible bugs in the control program, it is difficult to ascertain the source of errors.

In simulating the control program, it is necessary to imitate the functions of an entry block. Various artificial items, such as a message from a terminal, must be placed in the simulated entry block. The operational program has to be able to rent storage and obtain control information. Phase I must simulate all of the macros, and must act as if it is retrieving and storing records on the disks and drums.

At American Airlines, most of the testing made use of a simulation procedure which provided standard file records such as scheduled flights and passenger name records. A specially written debugging system was used for testing prior to the completion of the control program. This system, called SDP (Sabre debugging package), simulated all of the control program subroutines, the entry block, records going back and forth to the disks and drums, the activity of previous program segments, and the restoring of CPU registers after waits. SDP also provided debugging macros in the form of panel, core, disk, and drum dumps.

PHASE II

Here the actual control program is used with the disk files. No multiprogramming occurs. Input-output is by tape.

There are two parts to phase II:

(a) The testing of threads, one at a time.
(b) The tracing of different paths through each thread by using different entries.

Errors which occur in phase II testing may result from bugs either in the control program or in the operational programs.

PHASE III

Phase II is repeated, using more than one entry at a time for the same thread. Hence multiprogramming occurs.

The main problem in this testing phase is ascertaining which operational program causes an error. An error may also result from the control program.

Certain bugs may result from unique timing relationships which are not easily repeatable. The exact time when each entry obtains control of a machine facility depends upon the relative time each entry is introduced into the computer. It is also a function of such factors as the amount of movement required for access to records on tracks. Such timing relations among entries are difficult to repeat. Without the conventional debugging advantage of reproducing an error, real-time testing may become very difficult. Even the use of tracing as a debugging aid may change timing relationships. Hence, tracing may cause an error not to occur, or may introduce different errors.

PHASE IV

The entire system, including terminals and 7750's (if any), is tested by means of simulated inputs for a period of approximately 30 days. More than one thread is tested at the same time to ascertain whether there is interference among threads. Errors resulting from such interference tend not to be caught by the writers of individual programs.

In this phase, the system is tested with all queues loaded to capacity. Emergency programs are called upon whenever the limit of available core storage is reached. Phase IV tests whether these programs are operating properly, and whether the throughput rate of the system is adequate under these peak conditions.

The full loading of queues may require special testing facilities. In some systems, it may be possible to accomplish this by having one of the duplex computers feed messages to the other via one or more 7750's. Inputs to the 7750's may come from a special terminal set, or from tape. Another function of phase IV is to test the interworking of the central computer and the 7750 programs. Where bugs occur, it is necessary to ascertain which processing unit caused the error.

Various switchover procedures are tested in this phase. These include switchover from one CPU to another, switchovers between 7750's, tape unit switchover, and disk file switchover.

The handling of very long input messages is tested, as well as the treatment of invalid messages. File-maintenance procedures are also run in phase IV.

PHASE V

On-line terminals are gradually connected in this phase. In the early part of phase V, a single terminal introduces a short, one-thread test. Later, many terminals are connected for an entire day. Phase V should cause the rarest, most exotic errors to occur.

PHASE VI

Most of the records on the disks are actual rather than simulated records. The entries are real, rather than artificial. The number of terminals connected into the system for testing purposes is gradually increased during phase VI.

PHASE VII

Phase VII covers the period during which the system first becomes operational and in which bugs are removed in daily running, to the time when the system is running smoothly and when modifications are made. Modifications consist of adding new applications or making changes.

All changes should be tested on the backup computer before the programs are tested in actual real-time operation. It is necessary to provide methods for file protection when testing new programs, and to develop procedures for reconstructing files which are damaged during the addition of new programs.

PHASE I SIMULATION PROGRAM

Programs will not necessarily pass through all of these phases in a regular sequence. For example, if an error is found in an operational program in phase III, the program will be retested in phase I.

Phase I provides numerous debugging aids, such as selective dumping of parts of memory at designated times during the execution of the program. It is possible to place these aids in the phase I simulator.

Phase I uses five programs:

(1) A tape is maintained which contains a description of all test data to be used in phase I. A program is needed to create, update, and maintain this tape.

(2) The control program simulator performs the same operational functions as the actual control program. It calls upon the first program segment, and supplies it with the data it requires. The simulator links each program segment with other segments it may call upon, and provides the records which are requested.

(3) The data generator program is called upon by the control pro-

gram simulator whenever the operational program being tested requires a data record.

(4) A first-pass program is executed prior to the actual testing of any operational program. The first-pass program performs an initial check on the instructions in the operational programs to make sure that no restrictions or system requirements have been violated by the programmers.

(5) A librarian program is used to create and maintain a tape containing debugged subroutines, programs, and packages. At first all programs called upon by programs being tested are simulated. However, after a program has been debugged, it is placed on the library tape. The control program simulator now obtains these programs from the library tape when they are called upon by a program under test. The librarian program can patch, add to, delete from, or otherwise change any program on the library tape.

TESTING AIDS IN THE CONTROL PROGRAM

Certain testing facilities are built into the control program. These aids consist of memory prints. In the phase I simulation program, a memory print can be obtained at any point in the execution of a program. However, when an operational program is tested with the actual control program, memory prints can be obtained only at times when control is transferred to the control program.

An operational programmer can request a memory print of his program, the panel registers, his working areas, and his entry block. The programmer specifies what printouts he wants by control information included with his entries. Three types of memory prints can be requested:

(a) Memory prints for all programs that act upon an entry, whenever these programs yield control.
(b) Memory prints whenever a given program becomes activated.
(c) Memory prints of certain information placed on tape when programs yield control.

One of the testing facilities built into the control program is the *analysis block*. This is a block obtained by the control program from the available storage list. Each entry has an analysis block associated with it. As the entry is processed, the control program places memory print information into the analysis block. Whenever this block is filled, it is dumped on tape. The analysis block retains control bits which inform the control program what information to place in the block. Memory prints requested by operational programmers are obtained from the information dumped on tape from the analysis block.

A programmer can request three different types of debugging information when testing a program:

(a) A listing merely of the input and output messages associated with a given entry.

(b) A listing of the input and output messages associated with a given entry, along with a sequential listing of all of the departure macros (for yielding control) executed during the life of an entry.

(c) All of the information contained in (b), as well as the memory prints described previously.

ERRORS IN DYNAMIC PROGRAM MODIFICATION

The testing of more than one entry at a time helps to uncover violations of the program-modification rule. At one installation, as we have seen, operational programmers are prohibited from modifying a program if there is a departure macro between the modification and the execution of the program. The reason for this restriction in this particular system is that a program is not saved when it yields control to the control program. When the program is requested again, the control program always brings in the original version. Hence, a programmer must always assume that he will receive the original, unmodified version of his program when he rerequests its use. Programs are transferred into the execution area from upper core memory, or else they are read in from the files.

There is another reason for this rule. A small possibility exists that the very next entry which gets control may request the identical program which was just being used. If this happens, the next entry must obtain an original version of the requested program, not a version modified by the preceding entry. But in this case, the previous program still remains in the execution area.

THE DISCOVERY OF CIRCULAR HOLDS

Circular holds may be uncovered by testing more than one entry at the same time. The circular hold problem is as follows: Assume two programs are running simultaneously. Program 1 holds† record A, after which program 2 holds record B. Now suppose that program 1 requests record B for updating, and program 2 requests record A for updating. At this point, neither program can proceed further, for each requires a record which it cannot obtain, since each needs a record being held by the other.

No safeguards against circular holds were included in the American Airlines system. At another installation, a rule was established that an operational program is not permitted to hold a record until all records held across the last departure macro have been unheld. By unholding any records previously held, the program prevents itself from "locking horns" with another program. The testing of more than one thread simultaneously helps to ascertain if this rule is being violated. This testing, by the way, may also uncover situations where a programmer should be holding, and is not.

CONVERSION TO A NEW INSTALLATION

The converting of old procedures to a new data processing system involves great difficulties even in conventional batch-type installations. In a real-time system, conversion may present more complexities than testing. One problem results from the fact that terminals must be physically connected into a communication-based computer over a period of time. During this interval, unconnected offices must be notified by the computer when transactions are completed from on-line terminals. Similarly, transactions by off-line offices must be sent to the central computer and made available to the connected terminals. The large amount of additional communication complicates the conversion. Furthermore, the extra transmission may enlarge the burden on the system, thereby reducing its throughput speed during this period.

---

† As we have stated, the purpose of a hold is to prevent more than one program from updating the identical record at the same time. However, a second program may obtain a record held by a first program, if the second program does not intend to update that record.

12 THE OPTIMIZING OF SYSTEMS THROUGH SIMULATION

THE EFFECT OF QUEUES ON THROUGHPUT SPEED

Real-time systems must be designed so as to provide specified data services within a given time, at a minimum of cost.

The evaluation of computers and techniques for conventional batch-processing applications is based upon the time needed to execute the runs necessary to carry out the system's requirements. In a real-time system, on the other hand, there are no runs or passes. Information enters the system at random. More than one input is usually in the machine at the same time, thereby creating queues of transactions waiting to use system facilities such as the CPU and the disks. As the input load varies, the size of the queues becomes larger or smaller. Hence, estimates of efficiency and economy must take into account the effect of the various queues on throughput speed.

Here is a simple example of how queuing affects the operating characteristics of a real-time system: Assume a central processor connected to a number of remote terminals which transmit inputs to the computer for processing. After handling each transaction, the machine prints out an answer. The main processing center consists of a CPU, a disk file, a drum, and a printer. We refer to these units as "facilities" of the system. Let us assume that two types of transactions, T_1 and T_2, are entered from the terminals. Figure 12-1 shows a flowchart of the facilities employed by T_1 and T_2.

Both types of transactions initially require the use of the CPU for 5 milliseconds. A transaction T_1 next utilizes the drum for 30 milli-

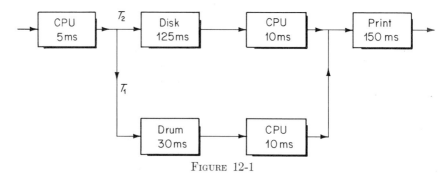

FIGURE 12-1

seconds. Then it uses the CPU again for 10 milliseconds. T_1 is printed during a period of 150 milliseconds. A transaction T_2 employs the disk for 125 milliseconds, the CPU for 10 milliseconds, and the printer for 150 milliseconds.

Let the system start operating at time t_0. Assume that a type T_1 transaction enters 2 milliseconds later at time t_2, and that a type T_2 transaction appears at time t_4. The history of the processing of these transactions is as follows:

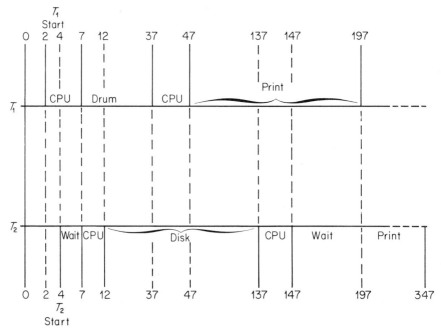

FIGURE 12-2

Transaction T_1 uses the CPU from t_2 to t_7, after which it employs the drum until t_{37}. It utilizes the CPU again until t_{47}. This transaction makes use of the printer during the period ending with t_{197}.

When T_2 enters the system at t_4, it must wait for 3 milliseconds until T_1 has finished with the CPU. Transaction T_2 terminates employing the CPU at t_{12}. It then uses the disk for 125 milliseconds and the CPU for 10 milliseconds. At t_{147} this transaction is ready to use the printer. However, it must now wait for 50 milliseconds until T_1 has finished using this facility.

Is the response time of this system adequate? To answer this question, we tabulate how long it took for each transaction to be processed:

Time for transaction T_1 = 195 milliseconds
Time for transaction T_2 = 343 milliseconds

We then compare these throughput times with the system's specifications.

ANALYSIS OF OPERATING CHARACTERISTICS

The time required to respond to an input depends both on the speed of the facilities and the length of time the transactions are forced to wait in queues. An analysis of the total throughput time is often very useful in locating the most significant factors. Here, for example, is a breakdown of response time into queuing and processing times:

Number of transaction	Actual time being processed	Queuing time	Response time
Transaction 1	195	0	195
Transaction 2	290	53	343

A more detailed breakdown would show specifically which facilities are responsible for the usage of throughput time. Such an analysis would enable system designers to ascertain what adjustments, if any, could reduce response time. In the above system, the longest delay occurs when transaction 2 waits for the printer. Hence, it might be advisable to employ a faster printer, or to use two printers. One of the most frequent bottlenecks results from the queuing of disk requests.

Numerous approaches to this problem can be considered. For example, it may be useful to reorganize the file structure or to utilize a drum.

A study of the operating characteristics of each facility also may indicate that certain units are overdesigned. When a facility is faster than necessary, it can sometimes be replaced with a less expensive unit. The following table describes the usage of units:

Facility	Percent of time busy	Percent of time idle
CPU	9%	91%
Drum	9%	91%
Disk	36%	64%
Printer	87%	13%

One way to avoid overdesigning a system is to run additional applications to keep idle units occupied. This is accomplished by keeping on hand conventional batch jobs with which facilities can busy themselves during lulls. However, whenever a real-time input enters the system, it must be permitted to interrupt the processing of the batch problem.

Priorities among transactions may have a significant effect. Where the high-priority records in a queue are processed first, this not only changes the response times to particular types of transactions, but also alters the entire structure of the processing.

MULTIPROGRAMMING SCHEDULING

During peak periods a large number of transactions are in a machine waiting to be processed. It has been suggested that optimization techniques would speed the operation of the system on such occasions. Such methods would be based upon a control program which would monitor and control the assignment of facilities to transactions. It is not always efficient to follow the first-come, first-served principle in processing inputs. In some cases, a certain type of transaction can be advantageously held up for a short period, in order to let its successors through. For example, in the above system, if another type of transaction were entered which required the use of the CPU for a very long period of time, all other inputs would be delayed greatly. An analogous phenomenon occurs frequently on narrow, winding roads, where a series of cars may sometimes be forced to crawl behind a slow truck for many miles.

One situation in which throughput minimization techniques might be profitable would be in a multiprogrammed computing center. In such an installation, a large number of programs stored on an operating system tape are always waiting to be processed. Here, the control program would seek to optimize the use of facilities by bringing the most expedient combination of programs into core at the same time. To achieve a maximum overlapping of I/O with CPU time, the mixture of programs brought into core for concomitant execution would be selected so that at least one of the programs would contain frequent I/O requests. On the other hand, the control program would avoid combinations of programs where each program required a great deal of I/O; with such a mixture, there would often be occasions when the CPU would be idle while all the programs awaited the completion of their input-output requests. If the system had 10 tape units, it would also be unwise for the control program to bring into core two or more programs, each of which required six tapes. With this mix, only one program could run at a given time. Similarly, if only 20,000 positions of core were available, the number of programs which could run simultaneously would be limited by the fact that they would have to employ a total of less than 20,000 locations.

Multiprogram scheduling at a computing center would require each program waiting to be run to contain a record of its characteristics. This description would include such data as core space required, number of tape units needed, some index of the frequency of I/O requests, and a rough timing estimate. The control program, or monitor, could then select in advance a mix of programs which would work together most effectively toward minimizing the joint throughput time.

One assumption implicit in scheduling is that there is no precedence relation among the programs; no one program depends upon another for its data. Optimization would be limited if the programs had execution priorities, for this would restrict the monitor from making many advantageous program mixes. By the way, scheduling requires all programs to be in relocatable form, for at compiling time it cannot be known where each program will be placed in core for execution.

Complete optimization would involve scheduling every program so as to achieve a minimum overall throughput speed. The monitor would seek to arrange the execution of programs so that, as each program terminated, it would be replaced by the successor most suitable for maximum utilization of the machine facilities. Such a procedure is similar to that used in *job-shop* scheduling, where a number of different operations must be performed in sequence on various raw materials by numerous types of facilities in a machine shop. In the job shop, the problem is to maximize overall throughput time by scheduling every job in advance so as to prevent excessive queuing and machine idle time. However, it is less practical to attempt overall optimization in multiprogram scheduling. The reason is that the amount of time each program will use the CPU and other machine facilities cannot be precisely estimated beforehand. Hence, it is difficult to devise a workable mix of every waiting program. Scheduling must probably be done with a short-range perspective, using only the current state of the system as the basis for selecting the next combination of programs to be concomitantly executed.

In a real-time system, multiprogram scheduling is possible only where transactions can be queued into batches. The optimization of machine facilities would also be possible if the central processor could partially control which inputs it received from the terminals. One procedure which might be feasible would be to schedule the items in a disk request queue so as to minimize the movements of the arm comb in accessing the desired records. In real-time applications, scheduling would have to be attempted only on a short-range basis, as the machine would presumably be unable to foretell appreciably its future inputs. If it proved feasible to gain time by scheduling transactions in any situation, this advantage would have to be weighed against the continual expenditure of time by the optimizing subroutine in the control program.

THE NEED FOR SIMULATION

The problem confronting designers of real-time applications is to devise the most economical system for responding within a specified time to fluctuating input loads. Although extensive work has been done in queuing theory, there is as yet no general mathematical procedure for optimizing a system configuration. Therefore, it is necessary to use trial and error methods. Systems must be studied with a varying number, speed, and arrangement of machine facilities. Numerous different methods for handling data must also be considered.

One way of designing a system would be to test it out on a small experimental model. For example, an automobile traffic control system could be studied by building a miniature network with tiny cars. The model would enable the observer to speed up or slow down the motion of these vehicles, as well as to reduce or increase their volume. Roads and traffic control facilities would also be varied to test out alternative configurations. The experimenter's task would be to prepare a model, set it in motion, and to observe its operating characteristics under different loads. By altering the variable factors in the model, the experimenter would attempt to arrive at an optimal system.

The use of physical models is usually impractical, for the systems to be designed are too complex to permit effective experimentation. A model is expensive to build, takes time to operate, and is difficult to use. Apart from these problems, so many tests may be needed to arrive at an optimal solution that it may not be possible to study the system by experimentation.

A GENERAL-PURPOSE SYSTEMS SIMULATOR

It is possible, however, to experiment with, analyze, and study problems in the design of real-time systems by creating adjustable models of the systems in computers, and by observing their operation under varying conditions. This *simulation* technique is used extensively in the development of optimal systems.

Many simulation experiments have been performed by employing special-purpose programs written by members of projects engaged in designing real-time systems. One of the first general-purpose simulators was written largely by S. A. Resnick and R. D. Villani of IBM research. A much more flexible and easier-to-use general-purpose simulator was afterwards developed by Geoffrey Gordon at IBM's Advanced Systems Development Division. We describe here the essentials of a simple version of the latter program.†

† Available from IBM through the DP Applications Library, No. 7090-CS-05X.

The user of the simulator first describes his system by a block diagram, which is coded into punched cards. With this information, he includes the speeds of the facilities and their storage capacities. The experimenter also specifies the transaction types and the load they place upon the system. The program's output consists of statistics on the information traffic, response times of the system, length of queues, percent utilization of facilities, and the use of information storage units. Priorities can be assigned to transactions and effects of peak loads can be studied.

The block-diagram model of the system consists of *nodes* or boxes each of which describes some action or characteristic of the simulated system. The sequence of actions is indicated by lines leading from each node to the next. Alternative courses of action are represented by having more than one line come out of a block. A choice of paths can depend upon mathematical functions or statistical probabilities. These decisions can also be based upon states of the system.

A variety of boxes are available for representing machine facilities in the system. The experimenter inserts special boxes to request various statistics from the program. Every box is numbered and contains information pertaining to the simulation. Often the time spent by a transaction in a facility varies between a range of values. This range is represented in the boxes by an average value called the *mean*, and by a positive or negative deviation from this average called the *spread*. When a transaction enters a box symbolizing a facility, the program chooses at random some value within this range.

The simulator operates by generating transactions and moving them through the model. The program keeps records of these actions and accumulates statistics. It not only observes how long it takes for transactions to pass through segments of the system, but also makes notes of the usage of information storage units. The simulator can therefore be employed to study both queuing time and queue-capacity problems.

The core of the simulation is a "clock" maintained by the program. This clock does not operate in real-time, but is advanced whenever a simulated event occurs. The program keeps looking for the next event due to take place. When it discovers the next happening about to occur, it moves this transaction forward in the model, and turns the clock ahead by the required interval of time.

THE SIMULATION OF AUTOMOBILE TRAFFIC QUEUES

The queuing of transactions in a real-time data processing system is in many respects similar to the congestion of automobiles at a toll station. In both instances, random inputs arriving at a facility cause the formation of waiting lines. Under peak loads, the throughput time of transactions, as well as cars, may become excessively long. Economic factors in both cases act as a constraint upon the addition of extra facilities to relieve the burden on the system.

To provide an easy illustration of the simulation of a queuing system, we present here, in Fig. 12-3, a simple example of how the general-purpose simulator program can be used to study the operating characteristics of three toll booths on a turnpike. We shall prepare a model of the following system, through which we will arrange for simulated cars to pass. We will give the simulator all necessary parameters relating to the traffic flow, and request the program to prepare certain statistics on the behavior of the system.

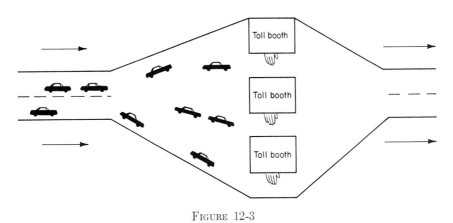

FIGURE 12-3

Examples of *originate* and *terminate* nodes employed in the automobile traffic model are shown in Fig. 12-4.

Originate box   Terminate box

FIGURE 12-4

The originate node is number 1 and the terminate node is number 18. In the originate node, the mean and spread are 4 and 4, respectively. These parameters cause successive cars to enter into the simulated toll installation within a range of 0-8 seconds after their predecessors. Where no figures for mean and spread are necessary, the expression 0:0 is placed in the node. At the terminate box automobiles leave the system.

Mark and *tabulate* nodes, shown in Fig. 12-5, request the program to obtain statistics on the time transactions take to move through specified segments of the model.

Mark box   Tabulate box

FIGURE 12-5

To indicate that a transaction is entering a memory unit, an *enter* box is used. A *leave* box symbolizes that the transaction no longer occupies this memory facility. (See Fig. 12-6.) In this example, automobiles are entering and leaving toll booths.

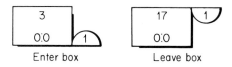

Enter box   Leave box

FIGURE 12-6

The number 1 in the attached semicircles designates the storage unit used by the transaction, i.e., the toll booth through which the car passes.

Branch boxes are logical devices for expressing several alternative directions a transaction may take. Figure 12-7 shows three possible routes which may be taken by automobiles.

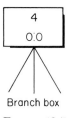

Branch box

FIGURE 12-7

When queues of transactions form, a *queue* node (Fig. 12-8) requests the program to keep a record of the maximum number and average number of transactions in this waiting line:

Queue box

FIGURE 12-8

The 2 in the circle attached to the queue box is the number of the queue.

A *seize* box indicates that a specified facility is now being utilized, and a *release* box causes the transaction to terminate its use of the facility. (See Fig. 12-9.)

Seize box   Release box

FIGURE 12-9

The 1 in the attached triangles refers to the particular facility (toll booth) being utilized. The mean and spread in the seize box are 15 and 4, respectively. This means that it takes an automobile between 11 and 19 seconds actually to pay its toll.

We will study the system's behavior under two different loads:

	Range of time between entrance of each successive car	Average time between entrance of each successive car
Load 1	0-8 seconds	4 seconds
Load 2	0-16 seconds	8 seconds

Figure 12-10 is the model of the three toll booths operating under load 1.

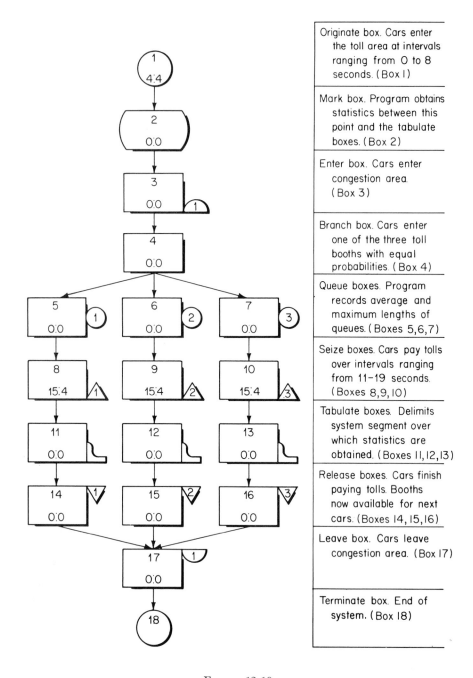

Originate box. Cars enter the toll area at intervals ranging from 0 to 8 seconds. (Box 1)

Mark box. Program obtains statistics between this point and the tabulate boxes. (Box 2)

Enter box. Cars enter congestion area. (Box 3)

Branch box. Cars enter one of the three toll booths with equal probabilities. (Box 4)

Queue boxes. Program records average and maximum lengths of queues. (Boxes 5,6,7)

Seize boxes. Cars pay tolls over intervals ranging from 11–19 seconds. (Boxes 8,9,10)

Tabulate boxes. Delimits system segment over which statistics are obtained. (Boxes 11,12,13)

Release boxes. Cars finish paying tolls. Booths now available for next cars. (Boxes 14,15,16)

Leave box. Cars leave congestion area. (Box 17)

Terminate box. End of system. (Box 18)

FIGURE 12-10

The program was requested to simulate the passage of 100 automobiles through the toll installation. Under load 1 it took 522 simulated seconds for this number of cars to pass through the system. Under load 2, 845 simulated seconds elapsed.

The simulator furnishes statistics on the length of time taken by every automobile in passing through each toll booth. In the case of toll booth 3 under load 1, one car took between 11 and 14 seconds to pass through the installation via this booth. Two cars took between 17 and 20 seconds. Twenty-two cars took more than 53 seconds to pass through the system. Figure 12-11 shows these statistics in graphic form. Thirty-four cars in all made use of toll booth 3. The remaining 66 automobiles employed booths 1 and 2.

Similar statistics were gathered for all toll booths under load 1. As in the case of toll booth 3, a large number of cars were held up for

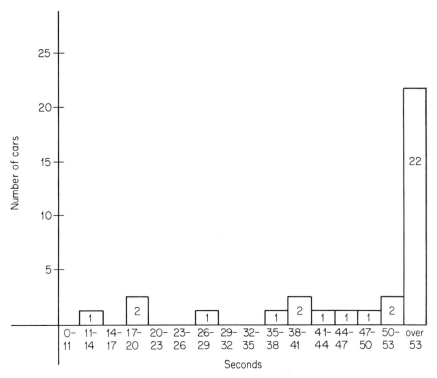

Time spent by automobiles in passing
through toll booth 3 with a load of 4:4

FIGURE 12-11

an excessive amount of time at the other toll booths. All of the booths operated at nearly complete capacity.

Toll booth	Fraction of time in use
1	.9981
2	.9923
3	.9636

Queuing statistics prepared by the program revealed that long queues were the source of the inadequacy of the system.

Queue at toll booth	Maximum number of cars in queue	Average number of cars in queue
1	7	3.0575
2	9	4.1437
3	6	3.1916

Simulation of the three toll booths under load 2 showed that the system is satisfactory when the average car enters every 8 seconds. Under this condition, only six cars took more than 53 seconds to pass through the system.

Utilization of the toll facilities under the lighter load was:

Toll booth	Fraction of time in use
1	.5432
2	.4675
3	.7586

Length of queues was as follows:

Queue at toll booth	Maximum number of cars in queue	Average number of cars in queue
1	2	.1408
2	2	.1586
3	4	.7929

USE OF THE RESULTS

This toll installation does not handle adequately an average load of one car every 4 seconds. Even under an average load of one car every 8 seconds, the system is somewhat unsatisfactory.

After ascertaining that a system is underdesigned, the experimenter varies the parameters in the model. In this case, he might increase the number of toll booths or their processing speeds. Then he simulates the system a second time and evaluates the statistics. The experimenter repeats this procedure until a satisfactory system is obtained. Of course, the parameters which he introduces must be technologically feasible and not excessively expensive.

As yet, there is no automatic method for evaluating the results of a simulation and for varying the relevant factors. Humans must analyze the statistics and devise new combinations of parameters. Possibly a future simulation program will examine its own results, try out different models, and converge upon an optimal system.

By the way, the above model of a toll installation requires certain additional features. For example, an actual automobile driver does not choose a toll booth at random, but tends instead to select the booth with the smallest queue. In a more realistic model, the route taken by each automobile is a function of the number of cars presently in each waiting line. This adjustment to the model could be made by instructing the general purpose simulator to make its behavior dependent upon the state of the queues. Such models may be necessary in the simulation of real-time data processing systems where the course taken by transactions is a function of the extent to which memory is utilized.

When using simulation, it is necessary to avoid certain pitfalls. Among these is the danger of studying a system before it reaches steady-state. Simulation begins before queues are present. In simulating the toll installation, for example, the program started with no vehicles waiting at the booths. This is unrealistic. At any given moment of time, there are usually a certain number of cars in various stages of passing through the tolls. However, in the course of a simulation it takes a while for the queues to fill up to a normal level. Only when this point occurs are meaningful observations of the behavior of the system possible. If data is recorded before reaching steady-state, the experimenter receives a biased picture of the system. In running a simulation, therefore, a user arranges to avoid recording the actions of the system until it attains a normal level.

SIMULATING A REAL-TIME SYSTEM

The general purpose simulator is in extensive use for the study of real-time systems. It is also valuable in the design of subsystems. One such use is the simulation of seek times to the IBM 1301 disk file.

We present here a simplified example of the simulation of a subsystem of an application in which a central office updates inventory records from shipment reports sent in from numerous warehouses. The machine configuration is as shown in Fig. 12-12.

The machine facilities perform these functions:

(1) Thirty input lines carry teletype information from terminals to the message exchange.

(2) The message exchange edits input messages in various ways. For example, it converts teletype code to 1410 code. Edited records are transmitted to the 1410.

(3) The 1410 initiates seeks to the RAMAC file. Upon the completion of input requests, the machine updates the records, writes them back in the RAMAC, and checks for accuracy of transmission.

(4) When the inventory drops to specified levels, the 1410 sends a message to the warehouses.

Simulation helped decide how many access arms to place on the RAMAC. The basic problem was the relatively long access time to the RAMAC file. These delayed the processing of inputs and caused queue formation.

With more access arms, access to the RAMAC tends to decrease. To obtain a record from RAMAC, an access arm must physically move to the disk containing the requested record. If the equipment includes two or more arms, these physical movements can overlap each other. In this

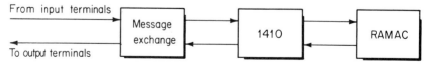

FIGURE 12-12

case, both seeks occur at the same time. This arrangement reduces the size of the disk request queue, and hence decreases the system's response time.

The designers analyzed RAMAC performance with one access arm and with three access arms. Frequency of input was based on an applications study which revealed that the machine installation would have to operate under three types of loads: normal, one-half normal, and maximum. The numerical values of these loads were:

Normal	6000 messages per hour
One-half normal	3000 messages per hour
Maximum	10,000 messages per hour

The time to complete a seek to RAMAC depends upon the distance of the access arm from the disk containing the information. The arm must move from its present position to the selected disk. Hence, fluctuations in access time will occur as a function of file organization and the frequency of seeks to various records.

Another variable factor in access time is the rotational delay before a record comes underneath the reading head on the access arm. To simulate these random fluctuations in accessing records, the experimenter instructed the program to use a table of mathematical probabilities.

The bar-chart in Fig. 12-13 displays the results of the simulations. Under a load of 3000 transactions per hour, the machine configuration with one RAMAC arm processed inputs at an average rate of about 0.54 seconds. With three arms, the rate was 0.45 seconds.

With a load of 6000 transactions per hour, the system with one RAMAC arm became overloaded. In this condition, inputs enter faster than the system can handle them. The queues become continually larger, and processing time longer. With three arms, the equipment handled 6000 transactions per hour at an average rate of 0.50 seconds.

Since the system overloaded at 6000 transactions per hour with one arm, there was no necessity for studying this configuration at maximum load, for the same problem of ever-increasing queues would obviously arise under this circumstance. With three arms and a load of 10,000 transactions per hour, the average processing rate was 0.58 seconds. The bar-chart in Fig. 12-13 displays average response times under the various conditions.

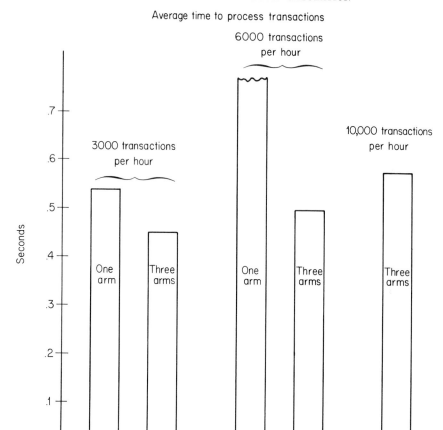

FIGURE 12-13

SIMULATION OF CHANNEL ASSIGNMENT

One installation used simulation to study how many disks and drums were best allotted to each channel to achieve optimum throughput speed.

This system utilizes IBM 7320 *need* drums. Each of these units is compatible with the 1301 disk file from a programming standpoint, and is exactly equivalent to the first outer ten 1301 cylinders. Eight 310-character records, or a total of 2480 characters are placed on each drum track. The shifting of records back and forth from the disks to the drums is valuable in fallback procedures. Since the average access time to a character on the 7320 drum is 8 milliseconds, it is planned to retain high-activity information on the drums.

Simulation indicated that where both disks and drums were assigned to the same channel, access to the drums was considerably slowed down because of the usage of the channel for input-output to the disks. For this reason, it was finally decided to put all of the drums on a separate channel.

SYSTEM DESIGN THROUGH SIMULATION

In designing a system, it may be found that equipment capable of adequately handling a peak load will not be utilized fully under normal circumstances. Under nonpeak conditions, equipment may even be idle a large percentage of the time. Overdesigned systems have a normal cost which is larger than necessary. Should a system be designed for normal loads or for maximum loads? If designed for peak loads, the installation operates uneconomically most of the time. However, if the system is built for normal loads, its operation may be unacceptable at peak times. In some situations, of course, there is no choice.

As a general rule, to ascertain whether a system is adequate, designers must determine the degree to which response times deviate from an average throughput speed. These data are part of the output of the general-purpose simulation program. It may not be necessary for all responses to occur in less than some stipulated time. Depending on the application, it may be tolerable for a certain percentage of transactions to be slower than specified.

A balance must be established between the cost of an installation and its operating capacities. Obviously, if enough money is spent, all systems can be made large and fast enough to handle any load. What is needed is an analysis of cost versus operating efficiency. At some point, a compromise between perfection and financial practicality must be made.

One of the practical limitations on the use of simulation in the design of real-time systems is that the values of some of the important parameters may be unknown in the early stages of design. For example, since the control program and the operational programs have not been written yet, the operating characteristics of these routines are conjectural. The designer must make guesses about CPU time, frequency of disk accesses, and the number of programs kept permanently in core. Even environmental factors may turn out to be inaccurate, for in converting to a real-time system, new procedures and methods may be instituted which change the number and size of the inputs.

At the outset, therefore, simulation may serve merely to provide a very rough guess as to the design characteristics of the system. Of course, the same problem of making accurate time and cost estimates has always been present in the installing of conventional data processing systems. But some estimate, however gross, is necessary.

The accuracy of simulation improves as programs are written and procedures become clarified or better understood. A real-time system requires simulation even at the time when it is about to become operational. At that time, certain decisions must be made which are possible only through simulation. For example, the decision as to how many operational programs should be kept permanently in core depends upon such factors as the expected amount of available core as well as the frequency and duration of requests for programs kept on disks or drums. Such trade-offs between space and time are an important part of the design of real-time systems.

INDEX